THE
BRITISH LIBRARY
PAST PRESENT
FUTURE

Front cover: The Double Helix, reproduced from an original painting by Peter Robinson.

Inside front cover: the staircase in Montague House, the first site of the British Museum. From a print c.1810.

Back cover: The opening page of the book known as the Sforziada, also discussed on page 56. A few copies, printed on vellum, were illuminated for members of the family by the painter Giovan Pietro Birago. The British Library has the copy for the head of the dynasty, Lodovico il Moro. The page illustrated has a border with portraits, coats of arms and emblems alluding to the family and its political power. The book was acquired by the Library with the collection of Thomas Grenville.

Text: R.C. Alston, assisted by specialists in all parts of the Library.
Photography: Anne Gilbert, Andrew Ogilvie, Chris McGlashon, Peter Sheppard.
Design: John Mitchell.

Published by The British Library
Great Russell Street, London WC1B 3DG

British Library Cataloguing in Publication Data

British Library
The British Library : past, present, future
1. Great Britain. National libraries : British Library
I. Title. II. Alston, R.C. (Robin Carfrae) 1933-
027.541

ISBN 0-7123-0196-8

Set in Monophoto Bembo type and printed in Great Britain by BAS Printers Limited, Over Wallop, Hampshire

Foreword

'Our purpose is to advance knowledge.'

Books are eloquent but rarely shout. How may we convey to those who do not know it well something of the rich and diverse collections of the British Library?

This booklet tells the story. Of necessity it uses many superlatives as becomes an organisation that in the range of its services is without a peer.

It is a Library for Great Britain and also for the world. It does not work alone but in co-operation with many other libraries, great and small, to advance learning, and to engage the minds of researchers and the community.

Those who work for the British Library are proud of its achievements and are ambitious to do better. Support from public funds and an earnings record beyond that of any other library help to ensure lasting achievement. The new Library now being built at St Pancras will offer much greater opportunities for exploiting the collections, presenting a unity of our diversity in humanities and science and enhancing our present and future services thereby.

We hope that those who read this story will find new ways of using and of promoting the British Library. It is our heritage: it is important for learning, and it offers enrichment for us today and for posterity.

Kenneth Cooper

Chief Executive

Artist's impression of the new British Library at St. Pancras seen from Ossulston Street. The new building will provide greatly enhanced facilities for the preservation of the Library's vast collections and their convenient use by all types of user.

Panizzi first sketched his design for the Reading Room on April 18 1852. The final design, by Sydney Smirke, the Museum's architect, was approved in January 1854. Work began in May, and the building was completed in three years at a cost of £150,000. The dome (140 feet in diameter) is just two feet less than that of the Pantheon in Rome. After it was opened on May 2 1857 the daily average of readers exceeded 400, whereas the reading room in use between 1838 and 1857 (pictured below) averaged about 180 readers.

The Unity of Knowledge

If the sum of human knowledge can be said to be found anywhere it would probably be in the British Library. Few libraries can match the richness and variety of its resources for research into every aspect of human thought and achievement. Its massive collections, and the use made of them, enshrine a principle as old as the first libraries about which we have any information – the unity of knowledge, and its power to transform. Books and manuscripts contain the DNA of civilization. Those who seek to understand the past and shape the future use the resources of the British Library in their thousands every day, from almost every country – by personal visit, by telephone, by post, and by internationally-linked computer networks. It is one of the world's very few general and universal libraries with sufficiently comprehensive collections to satisfy the specialist. Among the many communities of users served by the British Library are scientists, industrialists and businessmen, writers, teachers, academics in British and overseas universities, and hosts of individual researchers applying their initiative and energy to new topics of research. Remote users in all parts of the world rely on the British Library for information unobtainable elsewhere, and for services unavailable locally.

How did this come about? The British Library Act of 1972 was a public renewal of faith in the ideas which inspired the establishment in 1753, and growth over two centuries, of its oldest foundation component – the Library of the British Museum. The eminent doctor and scientist, Sir Hans Sloane, left his books, manuscripts, coins, drawings, and specimens of natural history and ethnography to the nation, to become the nucleus of the British Museum. Other collectors followed his example, and within a century the munificence of monarchs and the support of public funding had expanded Sloane's remarkable working library and 'cabinet of curiosities' into a great cultural and scientific institution. Within another century, further private benefaction and enlightened copyright deposit legislation had built up within this museum a library indispensable to the world of learning, and to those for whom information is a precondition of successful enterprise.

An institution may be created by Act of Parliament, but its potential can be realised only by the efforts of individuals. The reasons for the British Library's greatness lie not only in the foresight of the intellectual architects who gave the British Museum Library form and direction, but also in the ceaseless building up of its collections, whether by purchase, copyright deposit or donation, by generations of skilled and highly motivated staff. But knowledge of the past is only one dimension of understanding, and while the historical collections are undoubtedly important, the British Library has a commitment to the needs of those who shape the future. One phrase in the British Museum Act of 1753 has a permanent relevance – 'For publick use to all posterity'. It has taken two centuries to fulfil the grandeur of that promise.

Many of the British Library's treasures, on display in its exhibition galleries as well as accessible to scholars, are the gifts of generous collectors. Few libraries have benefitted more from the enlightened philanthropy of individuals who could depend upon a corresponding enthusiasm to preserve and make available to future enquirers the fruits of their endeavours.

Determination to provide ready access to information on every aspect of human thought and activity – cultural, scientific, technical and commercial – was the vision that led to the creation of the British Library in 1973, and it has now become not only a storehouse of the written record, but a vital repository of information serving the current needs of scientists, engineers, inventors, industrialists, lawyers and commercial companies, upon whose activities the economic strength of the nation depends. On a typical day the British Library supplies information to over 30,000 users: in the various reading rooms (which can accommodate 1450 readers), by post (letters, and requests for document supply as originals, microfilm or photocopy), by telephone (15 enquiry points), telex and online computer access. Of this total, a quarter are from outside the United Kingdom.

The Library which Sir Anthony Panizzi made famous in the middle of the nineteenth century – the Round Reading Room was opened to the public in 1857 – now has collections of over 150 million separate items housed in nineteen buildings in London and Yorkshire. In view of the enormous problems of continuing to satisfy the demands of its varied users from such dispersed collections, while ensuring that they are preserved for posterity, the plans for a build-

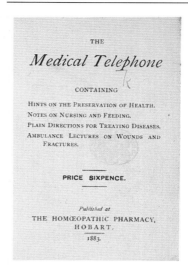

A *vade mecum* of home remedies, health hints, first aid, etc. printed at Hobart in 1883 which includes advertisements for a wide range of health care items, veterinary homeopathy, life assurance, ironmongery, a piano tuner, etc. from firms in Hobart, London and Manchester. A rare item, it was acquired by legal deposit in 1883. This is one among many examples in the British Library collections of material published in English from throughout the world. From 1842 the Act 5 & 6 Victoria, known as the Imperial Copyright Act, which specified that 'works sold, published, or offered for sale in any ... part of the British Dominions' should be deposited at the British Museum, was used to encourage administrators in British territories to pass legislation directing the local booktrade to comply. In the later nineteenth century when improved methods of book production assisted speedy dissemination of the printed word, the use of legal deposit, especially by North American publishers, was tested as a means of protection against literary piracy. Also important for the development of the English language collections from North America, Australia, Africa, the Caribbean, etc. was the printing at the end of the nineteenth century of the General Catalogue. Authors anxious to ensure immortality by having their works listed in what was then considered the foremost library in the English speaking world donated titles not already found in the catalogue. Scholarly publications not received by deposit, donation or exchange were purchased.

Sir Hans Sloane's magnificent collections laid the foundations for the great library of universal scope which Panizzi would later promote so energetically. Sloane's strengths lay in medical and scientific literature, so determining the Library's responsibilities towards the history of science. Later came Sir Joseph Bank's great natural history collections, and more recently the historical collections from the old Patent Office Library were incorporated. The riches of the English holdings in each are manifold, but enhanced beyond measure by those in foreign languages. The point is amply demonstrated by Godfrey Richards's translation of the First Book of Palladio's *Quattro Libri d'Architecttura*, the second edition of which (1668) helped to bring a 'second happy restoration' to the realm in the work of rebuilding after the Great Fire. Its influence can only properly be appreciated, however, in relation to the French and Italian originals from which it derives. The copy from which the engraved titlepage is here reproduced is itself a 'happy restoration', recently purchased to replace a copy destroyed by enemy action during the last war.

ing to accommodate most of the vast collections in London took on a new urgency.

Twenty years after its creation, political will, combined with a vision appropriate to the changing needs of its users, has ensured that the British Library will have a new home in London. The significance of the new building, the first phase of which is due to be opened in 1993, extends beyond the awesome statistics of its construction, and the magnitude, splendour and variety of the collections it will eventually house.

By bringing together on one site most of the Library's incomparable resources for the study of every subject – many of which have become dispersed in this century by lack of space in its London buildings – the British Library will be seen to be taking a leading role in facilitating the kinds of research and enquiry that future generations will require. But the concept of the new building lies not only in the bringing together of resources for all disciplines; it lies as much in providing new services made possible by advances in technology, and the provision of a physical environment constructed to ensure the preservation of the collections for posterity. Trusteeship of the past, and the present, has little meaning unless it can guarantee future benefits. The physician whose collections of printed books and manuscripts on all subjects, and in many different languages, formed the nucleus of the British Museum Library established a tradition that the British Library still honours, in giving access in one building to information on science and technology, as well as the disciplines associated with the humanities and social sciences. These facilities, and the services which will be provided, are without parallel in any other national library. The Library holds over 15 million volumes of printed books plus some 1.5 million cartographic items and music scores, and 8 million philatelic items. In the Newspaper Library are over .5 million volumes; the Western Manuscript and Oriental, and the India Office collections, totalling some 1.3 million printed books and manuscripts, are of international importance. The National Sound Archive contains .75 million discs. The magnitude of these collections is a source of great pride – pride which has to be matched with determination to achieve solutions to problems which libraries have never hitherto faced.

The Ashley Library, purchased in 1837, is one of the most valuable acquisitions of modern times. Formed by T. J. Wise, unfortunately also remembered for his thefts and forgeries, it contains many treasures of English literature, including a unique copy of Tennyson's *The birth of Arthur*. Byron's *Fugitive pieces*, his first book published in 1806, was afterwards suppressed.

Below: An opening from the interleaved copy of the first printed catalogue of the Library (1787) showing the holdings of Newton's works. By 1856 the catalogue had grown to 300 volumes, but by 1875 it had reached 2,250. Between 1880 and 1906 the process of transforming the manuscript catalogue to print was completed. The volumes in the Reading Room now number 2,008.

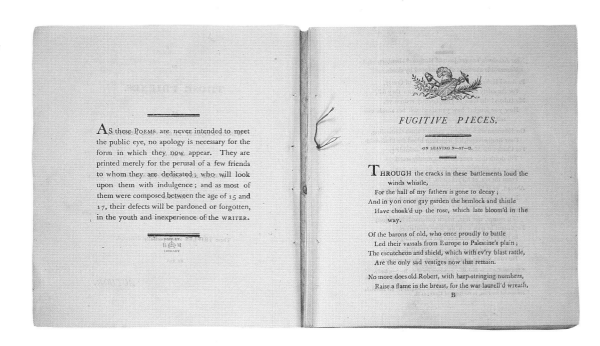

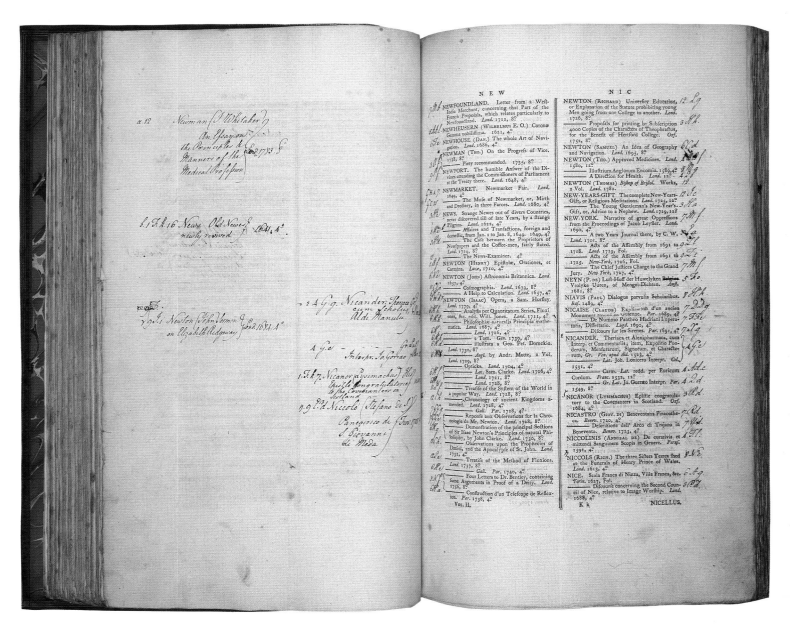

The Collections of the British Library

PRINTED BOOKS

From its inception in 1753 the Library has maintained an international as well as national purpose, through a policy of acquiring all materials associated with writing and printing. Printed books, in all languages, and on all subjects, have always formed the bulk of the collections, and now number more than fifteen million items. It has been estimated that the collections include books in over three thousand languages and dialects, some of which are now extinct.

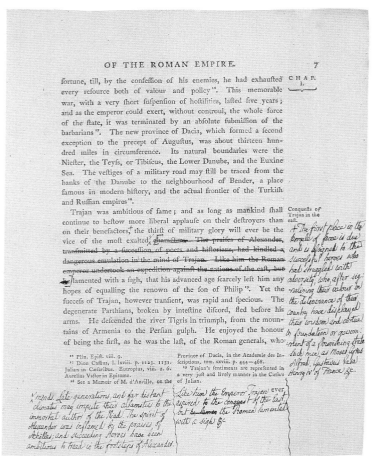

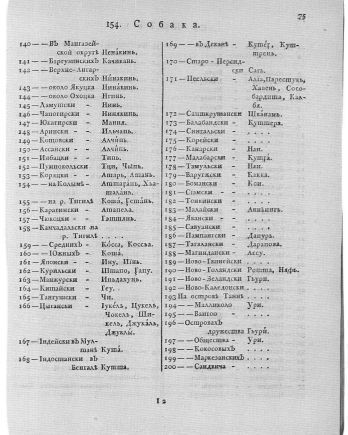

The Heritage of Empire

Books in English, the majority of which were printed in the British Isles, form the basis of the national printed archive which is augmented by books printed in all countries and dependencies formerly part of the British Empire, and in most of the languages of those countries. The Library continues to build on these collections and is one of the most important resources for the study of the languages and literatures of countries formerly under British rule. Publications in English derive not only from British colonies and dependencies persuaded to pass local legislation, which ensured that in addition to 'national' copyright deposit the British Museum Library benefited from 'colonial' copyright; but also substantial collections of books printed in English from Germany, the Netherlands, Scandinavia, Russia, China, Japan, Korea, Indonesia and the Philippines. The Library's collections of publications issued by governmental agencies within the 'Empire' was significantly enhanced in 1882, when the Treasury designated the British Museum Library as the recipient of documents received on exchange from foreign and colonial governments. Official publications, from all countries, account for a substantial proportion of the total number of items in the British Library, and cover legislation, the proceedings of legislative bodies, reports of government departments, statistics, and a mass of publications intended to be of help to citizens, as well as scholarly publications ranging

Far left: The British Library has incomparably rich variety in its collections of English books with distinguished provenances. Many – such as Gibbon's own annotated copies of *Decline and Fall* (far left) – are of acknowledged significance for the history of their texts, and the intellectual development of their authors. Others – such as Alexander Pope's own annotated copies of pamphlets written to attack him, or the numerous books formerly of Royal ownership in the foundation collections – constitute an important part of the national heritage, while offering fascinating glimpses of the intellectual development of their owners. For historians of the booktrade, or of particular manuscripts or copies of printed books, the Library has also especially valuable resources in the various series of English book-sale catalogues, a number of which are from the auctioneers' file sets, marked with prices obtained and purchasers' names.

Left: Peter Simon Pallas's multi-lingual dictionary *Linguarum totius orbis vocabularia comparativa*, (left) published at St Petersburg between 1787 and 1789. Here, the word for 'dog' is listed in two hundred languages. This copy, from the Banks collection, is one of very few Russian books in the early and foundation collections. Systematic acquisition of books in Russian began in the 1840s and the collections were subsequently built up by a succession of gifted linguists, scholars and Russophiles. By the end of the century the Library had the richest collection of Russian books outside Russia. Most material was acquired by purchase until the 1950s, when an extensive network of exchanges with Soviet libraries was set up. These exchanges enable the Library to obtain a wide range of journals, newspapers and monographs in all the languages of the Soviet Union. Emigré material is also collected, and the Russian and Soviet collections now number over 500,000 items.

Above: A hand-coloured woodcut portrait of the Czech religious reformer Jan Hus in the *Ivančice Hymn-book*, (right) printed at Ivančice in 1564 and produced by the secret press of the Unity of the Czech Brethren. Among the Unity's imprints, notable for their typography, decoration and standard of the Czech language, is also the six-volume *Kralice Bible* (1579-1593) which crowns the fine succession of Czech Bibles starting with the first Bible printed at Prague (1488), and the first illustrated Bible printed at Kutná Hora (1489). Antiquarian books of Czech provenance are complemented by extensive holdings of modern Czechoslovak publications acquired through a systematic acquisition programme.

The *Great Encyclopedia* of 1728 is a monument to official publishing in Qing dynasty China. Its Chinese title, *Gujin tushu jicheng*, means *Synthesis of books and illustrations ancient and modern*, and it is composed of excerpts from earlier works, selected by a team commissioned by the Kangxi emperor and completed under his successor, the Yongzheng emperor. The *Great Encyclopedia* took 27 years to edit, revise and print: its 800,000 pages bear more than 100 million characters and were printed with 250,000 pieces of copper type. It was by far the largest-scale work to be printed using copper types in pre-modern China. Although movable type printing was known to the Chinese as early as the 11th century, it never replaced woodblock printing as the principal means of printing. Sixteen years after the encyclopedia was issued, the copper types were melted down and made into coin. The British Library copy is the only complete set of the first edition outside China. It was acquired in 1877 through the British Embassy in Peking, who purchased it on the British Museum's behalf after protracted discussions with an impoverished imperial prince. Many volumes of the encyclopedia contain marvellous, detailed woodblock illustrations: the volume on sports and games, from which this picture of a football goal comes, shows acrobatics, exercises and more sedentary pastimes like chess and draughts. In the 18th century, when the encyclopedia was compiled, football had long ceased to be played, even as a court amusement, but existing descriptions were used to give an account of the rules of the game. In this picture, the names and positions of each player in the team are indicated between the two posts of the goal. From the banners, tassels and curtains which decorate the goal, it can be seen that Chinese football was a gentler, more refined form of the game than that we know today.

Wise women preparing herbs. From the only good copy known of the first *hortus sanitatis* in Polish, *O ziołach i o mocy ich* by Stefan Falimirz, printed at Cracow in 1534. The Polish collection in the British Library is believed to be the largest in Western Europe. It includes about 2,000 pre-1800 books (excluding works by Polish authors in Latin published in the West) some of which are very rare. Among them are 4 incunabula and 292 16th century books. Some of the most notable items are *Zwierzyniec* (1562) and *Zwierciadło* (1568) by the 'father of Polish literature' Mikołaj Rej, *Elegiarum libri IV* by Jan Kochanowski (1584), the 'Statute of Łaski' (1506), *Chronica Polonorum* by Maciej of Miechów (1521), *Historia Polonica* by Jan Długosz (1615) and the 'Third of May' Constitution (1791). Some categories of material are particularly well represented: early Bibles, legislation issued by the 16th-18th century diets, and Socinian literature published in Cracow and Raków between 1577-1638, some of which is very rare.

After 1800 the collection rapidly expanded, and is strong in 19th century material published in Poland and Western Europe and includes many first editions of 19th century classics, *Ksiegi narodu* by Adam Mickiewicz (1832) with a dedication in his hand, and the most translated Polish novel, *Quo vadis* by Henryk Sienkiewicz (1896), the first Slav Nobel Prizewinner for Literature among them. First editions of the works of the second Polish Nobelist (1924) Władysław Reymont, and most of the third, Czesław Miłosz (1980) are also held. The post-1945 part of the collection including material on the humanities and social sciences published both in Poland and the West is very strong. In 1988, 1,262 monographs were added to it and 19 newspapers, 130 periodicals and 306 serials were being taken. The most spectacular manuscript Polish items are two royal prayer books: that of King Alexander (1501-06), and Sigismund I (1506-48).

from ethnographical and archaeological reports to exhibition catalogues. International bodies are also strongly represented, with almost complete collections of documents issued by the United Nations and the European Communities, as well as many others from a host of bodies. The volume of official publications, British and overseas, available on loan from the Document Supply Centre is considerable. In the period since World War II, after which most of the former colonies gained independence, exchange agreements with other countries have ensured that the Library continues to acquire material it could not afford to purchase. The pre-eminence of the Library's collections of books printed in English is universally acknowledged.

The number of languages and scripts encompassed in the Library's Asian departments is startling. All the languages of the Semitic group (Arabic, Hebrew and Aramaic) are represented, and material in languages of the Turkic group, including Turkish and related languages spoken in a wide area of the Soviet Union and Central Asia continues to be collected. There are also rich collections of literature in all the Indian languages, classical and modern. All the languages of East and South-East Asia can be found, and these include many little known languages in addition to Japanese, Korean, Malay, Burmese and Thai. Here, a page from a 19th century manuscript produced in south-west China is reproduced. The script is known either as Lolo or Yi (the Chinese name for the group of languages spoken by a fiercely independent people who inhabit a remote mountainous area of Yunnan and Sichuan provinces). It is read vertically, starting from the top right. Linguists in China are currently working to map the dialectal variants of this language (currently spoken by about 5 million people) and to compare texts using different forms of Lolo script by looking at neighbouring and related languages in the Tibeto-Burmese family of languages to which it belongs. Texts like this religious manual of divination (in pre-modern Lolo society only religious leaders could read and write) were commonly added to the Library's collections by scholars and missionaries who shared a fascination for the history and ethnography of far-flung societies. Oriental Collections is the successor to the Department of Oriental Printed Books and Manuscripts, which was set up in 1892 to collect, catalogue and research Oriental subjects. It contains material in over 350 languages. The antiquarian material is complemented by growing holdings of modern publications and an important collection of newspapers from all over the world, including rare and early issues of newspapers from the nationalist periods of former colonies – some of them unique copies.

The World

The Library of the British Museum was not founded upon nationalistic principles: its main benefactors understood that knowledge does not belong to nations but to mankind, and that the benefits of what Locke called 'humane understanding' must flow to all. Such an ideal could scarcely be achieved by amassing a collection of books and manuscripts distinctively English. Sir Hans Sloane recognised this, and the bequest of his extraordinary collection of books, manuscripts and scientific objects enabled the nation to acquire remarkable items originating from the countries of Europe, Russia, Asia and China. The British Library has the earliest dated printed book, the Diamond Sutra found at Dunhuang (with a Chinese date equivalent to May 11th, 868 AD), as well as the most recent publications from places some might find difficulty in locating on a map of the world. A recognition that national boundaries, however politically important, should play no part in the policy of acquiring materials needed for the advancement of knowledge has resulted in a library which can provide access to the achievements of the mind, wherever those achievements have occurred, and by whatever means they have been transmitted. Neither do national boundaries affect the use which can be made of its collections, and the Library's users belong to all countries: many of them visit the Library to carry out their research; many more use its resources remotely, and the Document Supply Centre which holds a quarter of the total stock of printed volumes is one of the largest suppliers of information in print in the world.

'Animal Farm', a comic by Maciek Biały and Karol Blue [pseuds.], *Warsaw*, *[1985]*. The Library tries to keep abreast of current developments. Samizdat literature from Eastern Europe is collected and in 1984 the 'Works of George Orwell in the languages of Eastern Europe' exhibition was based on this material. In this category the most numerous are Polish underground publications which in January 1989 included 320 very incomplete titles of bulletins and periodicals and 285 books and pamphlets.

Poesie en diuerses langues sur la naissance de Henry de Bourbon, Toulouse, Iacques Colomiés, 1554. The British Library's French collections, containing over one million items, are the largest in the British Isles, and its holdings of pre-1850 French books are surpassed only by those of the Bibliothèque Nationale in Paris. The Old Royal Library and that of George III contributed many rare French works, and some important pamphlet collections were acquired in the 19th century, in particular the collections of polemical Mazarinades from the period of the Fronde, 1648-52 (7,000 items) and of French tracts of the Revolutionary period (49,000 items). Extensive use is made of the French collections of all periods by scholars and bibliographers searching for rare or unique items by major authors as well as more esoteric research material. An example of the latter is the work illustrated here, which is the only known copy of a polyglot verse tribute composed by the students at Toulouse University to celebrate the birth of Henry of Navarre, later Henry IV of France. One of the poems in this volume has aroused considerable interest among Breton scholars since its discovery by Library staff, as it is the first text in Breton to be printed with accents and is the only known sonnet in Middle Breton, with a complex pattern of internal rhymes.

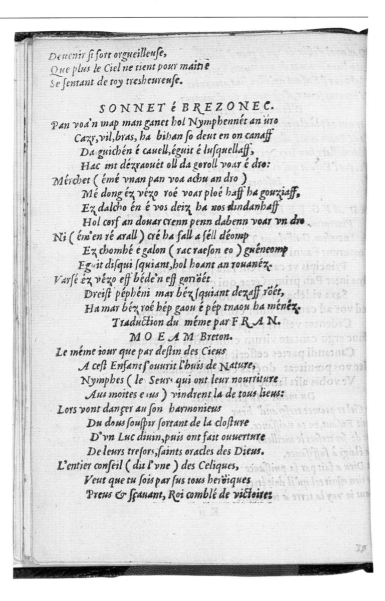

BOOKS AND DOCUMENTS FOR REFERENCE

The greater part of the printed book collections, in all forms, are available for reference and study in eleven reading rooms located in seven different buildings in London. Current research and information needs in the sciences, technology and commerce are provided in the three reading rooms of the Science Reference and Information Service [SRIS] at Southampton Buildings [UK and European patents, physical sciences and technologies, engineering, business information]; Chancery House [foreign patents]; Kean Street [life sciences and technologies, biotechnology, medicine, agriculture, mathematics]. A reserve store, with a small reading room, at Micawber Street houses older serials and books. The science collections cover all languages in which scientific and technical information is published, and is the largest and most comprehensive public library for science and technology in the world. In addition to books, serials, technical reports and indexes for every science, there are nearly 30,000,000 British and foreign patents. Users include information officers, researchers, postgraduate students, academic staff, abstractors, technical journalists, industrial managers, librarians, patent and trademark agents. The majority of users come for current information from its huge resources for science, technology and commerce, and SRIS provides a wide variety of essential reference tools in printed and electronic form. The special information services provided by SRIS for business, Japanese technology, and biotechnology have required considerable investment in new technology, and an increasing number of requests for information require access to hundreds of scientific, technical and commercial databases. As the national library for science and technology SRIS will, when it moves to the new building at St. Pancras, fulfil one of the prime objectives in the creation of a British Library: to give substance to the belief that the economic future depends upon science and technology, as the cultural future depends upon an understanding of the past.

The Science Reference and Information Service (SRIS) is the national library for modern science, technology, and commerce, and also for industrial property including trade marks and designs. It has an unrivalled stock of reference books, journals, patents, and other printed sources of information; and it also offers photocopy and information services. The collections are the most comprehensive of their kind in Western Europe, with a stock of more than 270,000 monograph and serial publications and 29 million patent documents from all over the world. The literature is available on open access and is complemented by expert assistance from the reading room and information services staff. Entrance and use of the collections is free, whilst a charge is made for photocopying and information services, for seminars on various aspects of information and for publications produced by SRIS staff or through collaboration with outside organisations. The illustration shows the main Reading Room at Holborn where literature on engineering and the physical sciences and technologies is held, together with business information and British and European patents. An adjacent building houses the foreign patents collections and reading room; and at the Aldwych reading room are held the collections in the life sciences and technologies, especially biotechnology, medicine, agriculture, and mathematics. Items held in remote store in London can be brought to the reading rooms within an hour or two, and SRIS works closely with the Document Supply Centre at Boston Spa to satisfy reader requests which can be met by each from the other's collections or information services.

A patent agent examining the patent for Koenig's perfecting machine which was used to print the London *Times*. The first book to be printed using this machine is illustrated overleaf.

The Great Exhibition of 1851 demonstrated the power of invention and technology to change the world, and of trade to provide the economic basis for Empire. The establishment of the Patent Office Library in 1855, under the vigorous leadership of Bennet Woodcroft (inventor of the variable pitch screw propeller), was a landmark in the history of libraries in Britain, for it was the first public library to offer free open access to its collections: a tradition still maintained. The purpose behind its creation was expressed simply as the provision of materials 'indispensable to the right direction and advance of British industry'. The visionary Woodcroft would be pleased that the institution he shaped is now part of the British Library, and that its collections have expanded to include trade literature – catalogues, data sheets, price lists, house journals, company annual reports, stockbroker reports, product literature of 30,000 British and foreign companies, market research reports, business statistics, etc. – as well as monographs and serials on every science, and patent specifications from every country.

As a country whose cultural and intellectual history has always been inextricably involved with the countries and empires of continental Europe, it is hardly surprising that from the beginning the enrichment of the national collection of books printed in those countries was regarded as a priority. After two centuries of enlightened acquisition and benefaction there is no country in Europe that can chronicle adequately its history without recourse to the British Library. From the beginnings of printing in Europe to the year 1500 there is not one place where printing has been recorded that is unrepresented in the collections, and for succeeding centuries there are probably few places in which printing is known to have existed for which examples cannot be found in the collections of the British Library.

The importance of the collections for French, German, Italian, Spanish, Portuguese and Dutch history and literature is a reflection of the role these countries played in bringing about that enlightenment which has created modern Europe, as well as the fundamental role of economic development through trade. The collections of books in the major European languages are so extensive that the specialist catalogues which the Library has published are regarded

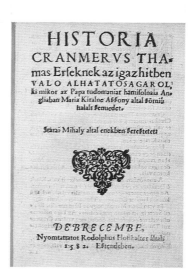

A unique copy of the narrative poem by the 16th century Hungarian dramatist Mihály Sztárai, celebrating the life and martyrdom of Thomas Cranmer. The foundations for the Library's immensely rich holdings of Hungarian printed books were laid early in the 19th century through energetic pursuit of Panizzi's bold and imaginative collection development policies. Later in the century, from the libraries of two Hungarian bibliophiles István Nagy and László Waltherr, unrecorded 16th century imprints were added, as well as many rare 18th and 19th century pamphlets on the literature and history of Hungary. Today the Library strives to acquire all key works from Hungary in the humanities and social sciences, together with Hungarian publications from neighbouring East European countries.

Schiller's *Das Eleusische Fest*, London: Bensley & Son, 28 Feb. 1816. The first product of the first perfecting machine, on which both sides of a sheet could be printed in one continuous process, invented by Friedrich König and Andreas Bauer. There are introductory verses by them on the benefits of British technology and the German invention of printing. A dedication copy by König, acquired in 1977. The patent for this machine is in SRIS and is illustrated on the previous page. The British Library holds one of the world's greatest collections of books from the German-speaking countries, from all periods and on all subjects, and includes much that is rare and unique. While additions are regularly made to the earlier holdings, the main aim of the acquisitions programme is to cover all current literature of scholarly importance.

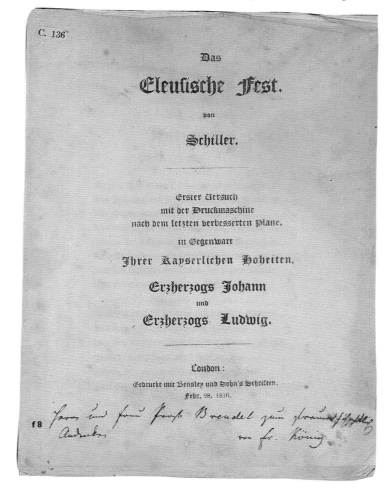

Patent literature reflects the almost limitless diversity of human inventiveness, although many applications for a patent may never reach the final stage of being granted and published. Most of those that do will probably not achieve significant commercial success, but the collections in SRIS do contain some patents which can rightly be regarded as historic. The illustration shows a page from a British patent granted in 1952 to Chester F. Carlson, an American working in the patents department of a New York electronics firm. He had become frustrated by the difficulties of obtaining copies of patent documents and had experimented since 1934 with electrostatic copying, as outlined in the patent shown. The process, now known worldwide as xerography, was not an immediate success. More than twenty firms turned down Carlson's efforts to develop his invention. Finally, in 1944 the Battelle Memorial Institute, a non-profit industrial research organization, intervened. In 1947 the Haloid Company of Rochester, New York acquired the patent rights and subsequently became the Xerox Corporation. Eleven years later the first office photocopiers were marketed. Today, however, there should be no difficulty in getting copies quickly. SRIS holds the world's greatest collection of foreign patent specifications and related literature, and its Photocopy Service supplies over 500,000 items annually.

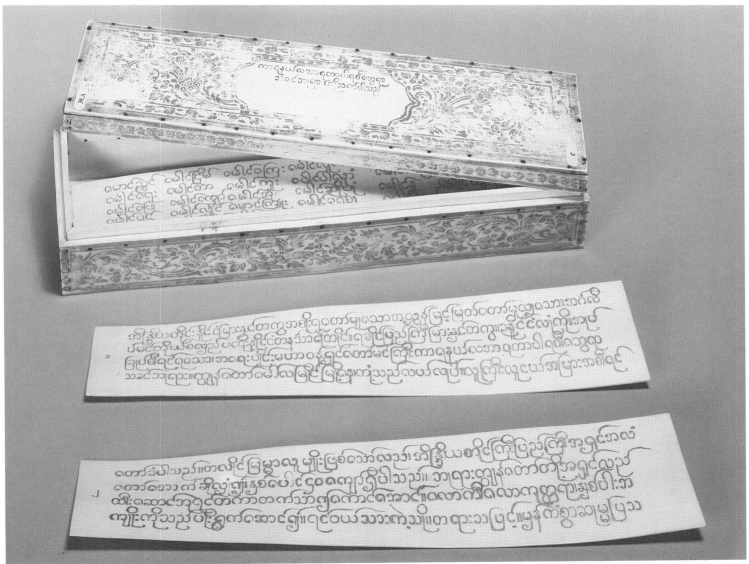

Farewell memorial presented to Sir Arthur Phayre, Chief Commissioner of British Burma, in 1867 by the inhabitants of Moulmein. On seven ivory sheets with text in gilded Burmese script, and contained in an ivory case ornamented with gold floral designs and the name Colonel Arthur Purves Phayre in Burmese characters.

Manuscripts from Southeast Asia come in a variety of shapes and forms: beautifully illustrated folding books from Burma and Thailand; Court histories from Java with richly decorated frontispieces; delicately illustrated palm leaf manuscripts, often with carved wooden covers; while bamboo, tree bark, ivory, gold and silver have also served as media for the written word.

as indispensable sources in the countries to which they pertain. Excellence in scholarship in all disciplines builds on the best available research irrespective of language, and the Library acquires current publications from abroad on this principle.

The languages of the Indian sub-continent, as well as many other oriental languages, are represented in two major collections. The India Office Library was founded in 1801 as a public repository for its books by the East India Company whose original charter in 1600 gave it trading rights from the borders of the Ottoman Empire to the Pacific Ocean, including southern Africa, the Arabian Gulf, Indonesia, Malaysia, Singapore, China and Japan. The resources of this library are complemented by those in the collections in the Department of Oriental Manuscripts and Printed Books (now known as the Oriental Collections), established within the British Museum in 1892. Together, these two collections form the largest and most important body in the world for the study of Asia.

The printed books in the Oriental Collections, as distinct from those in the India Office Library, had their origin in the foundation collections of the Sloane and Harleian libraries. For a century, the most important acquisitions were those of manuscripts – the collections of Claudius Rich purchased in 1825, and William Erskine donated in 1865. In 1867 the Oriental manuscripts totalled some 7,000 volumes, and a subdivision of the Department of Manuscripts was established. Today the Oriental Collections in Store Street have printed books in over 350 languages, or language groups, for the whole of Asia from the Mediterranean to Japan, North and North-East Africa, and represent the traditions throughout the world of Jewish, Christian, Muslim, Hindu and Buddhist religions. The catalogues of these collections frequently constitute the definitive bibliographic authority for the literatures they cover. Current acquisition policy aims at maintaining a comprehensive library of writings in the indigenous languages of North Africa, Asia, China and Japan not only for their content, but for their material form as evidence for the 'history of the book'.

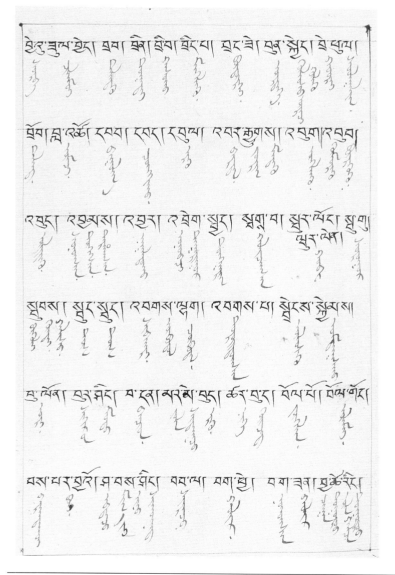

A Tibetan-Mongolian vocabulary (late 19th century), with preface in Mongolian. The Tibetan books and manuscripts held by the India Office Library and Oriental Collections together constitute the largest such collection in the West, and the most important anywhere to which scholars have free access. Oriental Collection's rich inheritance from the British Museum includes a history of Tibet known as the *Green Annals*, a rare work, one of the few known to have been composed by Mon-pa, written by or for the Sixth Dalai Lama in 1701; a unique set of musical scores in Tibetan musical notation; and a manuscript copy of the *Kanjur* in 106 volumes, probably 15th century, which has been shown to derive from a lost Sanskrit original pre-dating the Narthang and other extant printed editions. Other manuscript treasures in Oriental Collections relate to outlying regions of Tibet including Ladakh, Nepal (Lepcha), Sikkim and of course China. In addition to Buddhist literature which of course predominates, an important number of Bon-po text represent the autochthonous religion of Tibet – particularly since the purchase in 1983 of the collection of twenty such manuscripts formed by Professor David Snellgrove.

Whereas a sizeable proportion of Oriental Collection's Tibetan manuscripts and blockprints had been 19th century accruals to the British Museum, the India Office Library had little to show by 1900 other than the block-printed copies of the *Narthang Kanjur* (105 volumes) and *Tanjur* (223 volumes) presented by B. H. Hodgson, British Political Resident in Nepal. Both Libraries however were donated equal shares of the large and choice collection brought back by Lt-Col Waddell from the Younghusband Mission to Tibet. Waddell's generous gift virtually founded both collections as they stand today. A near-complete *Narthang Kanjur* (96 volumes) and beautifully written in the India Office Library are among the finest treasures associated with that unfortunate political venture.

The collections have not stood still since Waddell's time. Among recent major purchases is the magnificent 17th century yellow silk edict announcing the appointment of Kalsang Rabje as Secretary to the Dalai Lama and bearing the seals of the Dalai Lama, the governemt of Tibet and of the Chinese representative.

BOOKS AND DOCUMENTS FOR REMOTE USERS

The requirement to maintain a national reference library which would serve as a preserved archive of the history of writing and printing is one that most countries accept; but as long ago as 1850 Panizzi recognized the parallel need to supply books to readers on loan. The development of public libraries was firmly involved with the Victorian concept of progress, but whereas the spread of public lending libraries, serving local communities, grew rapidly after 1852 (the year in which the Manchester Free Public Library was founded), it was not until 1962 that Britain acquired what no other nation has: a lending library which serves the research needs of industry and commerce, universities and polytechnics, government departments, institutes of research and public libraries by loan of originals or photocopies. Most of the users of this unique resource for printed information – the Document Supply Centre at Boston Spa – come from industry and commerce, and the largest proportion of the holdings

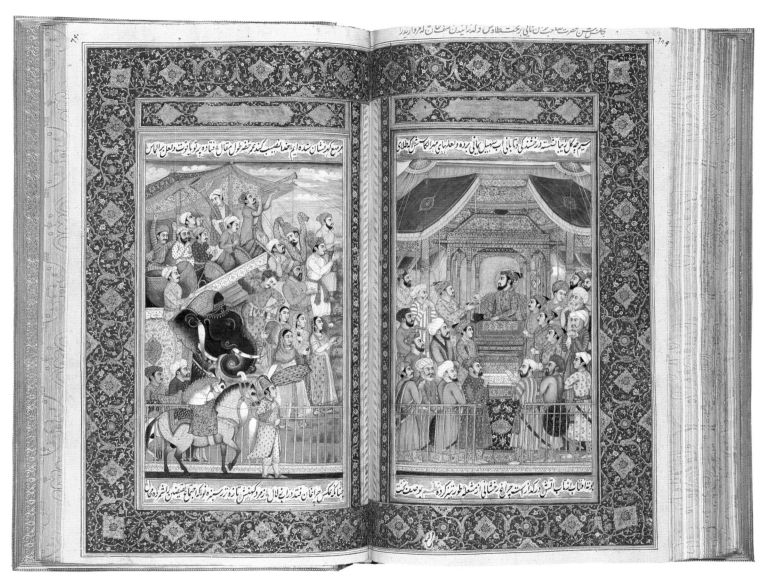

The Mughal Emperor Shāh Jahān is presented with pearls as he celebrates his accession to the throne. Miniature painting from a manuscript in Persian ʿAmal-i Sālih, a history of Shāh Jahān's reign by Muḥammad Sālih Kanbū. Taken together, the Persian manuscript collections in the Library represent one of the largest and finest in the world. This applies especially to the fields of *belles lettres* and history, and also to all branches of traditional literature and science. Persian literature has been transmitted not only from Iran and Afghanistan but also from Central Asia and the Indian subcontinent. The Turkish collection, too, is a rich treasury of rare texts, including the poetical and other manuscripts of E. J. W. Gibb, the historian of Ottoman poetry; and, from much earlier times, Turkic manuscripts and

fragments brought by Sir Aurel Stein from Eastern Turkistan. An outstanding feature of the Persian, Indo-Persian and Ottoman Turkish collections is the range and number of miniature paintings, many of them in rare styles. The holdings of antiquarian printed materials are likewise extensive, and particularly strong in early Indian imprints. There is a specially-bound collection of Ottoman photograph albums and books presented in 1893 by order of the Sultan. The Library acquires most significant contemporary publications in Persian, Turkish and related languages in the humanities and social sciences. As Turkey's links with Western Europe grow stronger, the importance of the Library's Turkish material is becoming recognised.

represents the sciences and technology. A quarter of the 3,000,000 annual requests for document supply received at Boston Spa come from overseas. In spite of the fact that the majority of the users request current or recently published material, the collections at Boston Spa cover all subjects and periods, and there are substantial numbers of early printed books in all languages. The very substantial holdings of eighteenth- century English items are now recorded in the internationally supported Eighteenth-Century Short Title Catalogue project. The holdings of nineteenth-century English books are particularly impressive, and include thousands of rare items which are available on loan to other libraries.

The largest proportion of the printed books at Boston Spa is serial publications, covering all subjects, and in all the major languages. In 1988 an ambitious programme to convert the records for all current serials to machine-readable form was completed, thereby enabling rapid and efficient incorporation of accessions. In the same year the Library launched the Adonis Project, a document delivery service for articles in over 200 biomedical journals held on CD-ROM and capable of producing on demand articles in hard-copy form for research. The file is updated weekly and copies of the new disks are sent to the other participating document supply centres in Paris, Madrid, Stockholm, Amsterdam, Cologne, Berkeley, Ann Arbor, Monterrey, Canberra and Tokyo. The specifications for the Adonis workstation were drawn up by the British Library.

The monograph collection exceeds 3,000,000 titles (in a wide variety of languages including Chinese, Japanese and Korean), and is added to every year by over 50,000 acquisitions and donations. In addition, Boston Spa holds over 500,000 translations; 250,000 conference proceedings; 300,000 reports; 500,000 American dissertations; and 75,000 U.K. doctoral theses. Bibliographical records for a substantial number of items held at Boston Spa are available on-line.

Because the volume of requests received at Boston Spa is so considerable (1,250,000 per annum in 1973, over 3,000,000 in 1988), and because of the requirement to satisfy requests in the shortest possible time, automation has been given high priority. In addition to optical disk storage of the text of biomedical journals, the Document Suppply Centre now handles almost half of its requests by sophisticated telecommunications equipment. An Urgent Action request from anywhere in the world can be responded to within hours using telefax (Group 3 is standard, but in 1988 the Library introduced new high-quality Group 4 equipment).

The benefits to research, and thereby economic and social prosperity, which depend upon the availability of the information to be had from the vast collections of the Document Supply Centre can hardly be over-estimated. No other library can claim to furnish on such a scale the printed materials for an understanding of the past and the present.

MANUSCRIPTS ARCHIVES AND RECORDS

The manuscript collections of the British Library are to be found on four sites: in Bloomsbury, Store Street [the Oriental and Philatelic collections], Orbit House [the India Office Records], and Southampton Buildings [SRIS]. Taken together the collections form one of the largest and most important repositories of writing in the world. Almost every known language is represented, as well as almost every material on which writing has been found.

The Department of Manuscripts was one of the three original departments of the British Museum. When the Museum opened in 1759 the manuscripts came from the Cotton, Harley, Sloane and Old Royal libraries. They included manuscripts in the languages of the Ancient World, the Near and Middle East, Western Europe and the Orient: Greek and Latin papyri, Biblical codices, medieval manuscripts from all over Europe, post-medieval historical papers, literary autographs, music, maps, plans, topographical drawings, charters and seals. For the history of art, the illuminated manuscripts which formed the basis of the foundation collections include masterpieces like the Lindisfarne Gospels from the Cotton library. Of the many manuscripts which shed light on the history of Christianity two are of fundamental importance: the Codex Sinaiticus (ca. 350 A.D.) and the Codex Alexandrinus (ca. 425 A.D.). The collections have been added to by purchase and donation and now number over 150,000 volumes in over fifty languages.

When the Museum established a department for the oriental collections in 1867 it recognised the importance of entrusting to specialists an unrivalled resource in Europe for the historical study of the civilisations of North Africa, the Near and Middle East, and Asia. As with the collections for the history of Western civilisation there are items of extraordinary importance for the origin and development of writing and printing (the Chinese oracle bones date from

When speed is absolutely essential to the success of a project, the Document Supply Centre can provide special services to help its customers. The Urgent Action Service is both quick and inexpensive – customers phone in their requests which are processed within two hours and despatched the same day by fax (pictured above), courier service or first class post. Using the Urgent Action Service means that the customer is notified quickly if a search has been successful or not. The Centre also offers a service which saves time and effort by enabling the customer to send complete lists of references together, to be processed as a batch by one person. The Reference Listing Service can accept typed lists or computer printout and sends satisfied requests in one package via overnight courier just two to three days after receiving the list.

Also pictured (right) is an area of the Document Supply Centre's storage facility. The total amount of stock is held on over 100 miles of shelving and contains 7 million books, journals, reports and theses, covering almost every subject in any language: continually added to every day of the year from a budget of £4 million. Advanced systems ensure that customers receive the documents they request, normally within 48 hours. Over 3 million requests are received each year: 87% are satisfied from the Centre's own stock. With over 30 requests every working minute and 12,000 items despatched each day the Centre operates with the efficiency of the best run, conventional mail order houses – quite unconventional for a library! Pictured below is the despatch area where items are sent out by various means such as first class post, courier and the Interlibrary Transport scheme network.

the second millenium BC, while the Buddhist charms printed in the reign of the Empress Shotoku date from about the year 765 AD). The illuminated manuscripts form perhaps one of the richest sources for the history of Judaic, Muslim, Buddhist and Hindu painting.

When the custody of the India Office Library and Records was transferred from the Foreign and Commonwealth Office in 1982 the British Library acquired responsibility for one of the oldest research institutions in Europe, for the records of the East India Company (1600-1858), the Board of Control (1784-1858), the India Office (1858-1947) and the Burma Office (1937-1948) constitute an immensely significant part of the public records of the United Kingdom, and the largest part of those records outside the Public Record Office. They tell the story of how a private mercantile trading company came to rule the whole Indian sub-continent and associated areas in Asia, which later became the direct responsibility of the British Government and the 'jewel' in its crown. These official records are supported by thousands of ship's journals and logs, private papers and correspondence and the records of baptism, marriage and death for thousands of Christians across Asia. All this, and large numbers of manuscripts from and relating to the countries of what used to be called Hindustan – modern India, Pakistan, Bangladesh, Nepal, Sikkim, Bhutan and Sri Lanka.

One important part of the manuscript collections is the Archives which, in addition to the Trustees' documents in the care of the British Museum, constitute an invaluable record of the history of the Library and its collections. Unlike the records of British rule in India and the Patent Office Library, which form the core of the archives in Orbit House and Southampton Buildings which are freely available, access to the archives of the British Museum Library to 1973, and the British Library thereafter, is restricted in that prior appointment must be made before they can be consulted. They represent a documentary resource of considerable importance for the history of librarianship.

A selection of the ingenious use of materials included within the omnibus term 'manuscripts'. In addition to the more familiar papyrus, vellum and paper, these embrace palm-leaves from South and South-East Asia, bronze land charters from India, oxbone from China, wooden envelopes, bamboo letters and stone inscriptions. These different mediums are important as they are often responsible for the development of specific forms of script; for example, producing curvilinear writing on fragile and grained palm-leaves, or monumental letters in response to the texture of metal or stone. Metal seal dies are also included in the Library's collections, as are the wax seals themselves and impressions of both produced in rubber or plastic. Each type of material has its own storage requirements leading to equally imaginative solutions on the part of Preservation Service regarding their protection.

The birth of Julius Caesar, from a manuscript produced at Bruges in 1479. Contained in the Royal Library which George II presented to the nation in 1757, one of the foundations on which the British Library's collections are based, are manuscripts collected by Edward IV which form the earliest evidence for the formal collecting of books by an English monarch. Each of these very large volumes contains French texts written and illuminated in the Low Countries following tastes developed at the Burgundian court, to which Edward was closely linked. They were intended for the lectern, their texts to be heard and pages admired. This manuscript is typical, and bears Edward's heraldic devices. More important perhaps is the fact that it alone mentions Edward IV by name, recording that the principal text, a revised version of a medieval biography of Julius Caesar, was executed for him at Bruges in 1479.

Left: A page from the Barcelona Haggadah, a fourteenth century Hebrew manuscript copied and illuminated in Northern Spain. Here the father breaks the first Matzah at the beginning of the Passover ritual. The Hebrew Collection of the British Library contains nearly 3,000 manuscripts, including many Bibles and service books, also philosophical, mathematical and medical works. Among them are some of the finest examples of Hebrew book illumination, as well as a number of legal documents pertaining to the Jews of England in the thirteenth century. In addition to these manuscripts, there are 10,000 fragments, most of which come from the store (Geniza) in the Synagogue of Old Cairo in Egypt. They tell us much about history, trade and daily life around the Mediterranean in the Medieval Period.

Apart from the manuscripts, there is a very large collection of Hebrew and Yiddish printed books, periodicals and newspapers (c.60,000). They cover a wide range of subjects including Bible studies, history and the Holocaust, the geography of the land of Israel, politics, archaeology, economics, sociology and law.

Right: Samuel Taylor Coleridge's 'Kubla Khan', among the most famous and important items in the British Library's rich collection of manuscripts of the Romantic movement. This is the only surviving copy of Coleridge's well-known poem, made for an admirer at some time between 1797, the year in which it was composed, and 1816, the year in which it was first published at the suggestion of Lord Byron. Coleridge described it at different times as 'a psychological curiosity' and a 'fragment ... composed in a sort of Reverie brought on by two grains of Opium'. It is made up of a series of haunting visionary images, suggesting grand themes of eternity and change. He was unfortunately interrupted, in the process of writing it down, by the arrival of a 'person ... from Porlock' (a nearby village in Somerset), who broke the creative spell.

Benedictine nuns of the Abbey of Maredret, near Namur, illuminated this leaf of the Pastoral Letter of Cardinal Mercier, Christmas 1914. The decoration is adapted from 14th century French work, the miniature of Habbakuk feeding Daniel represents

America's aid to starving Belgium, and the American flag is displayed in the left margin. At the foot of the page the Allied fleet, in mediaeval guise, confronts the Germans at the first battle of the Yser.

Bound in gold, with rings by which it could be suspended as a jewel at a lady's girdle, this miniature volume contains a portrait of Henry VIII after the image of Holbein. The text is an English version of the penitential and other psalms by Master John

Croke, one of the six Clerks in Chancery in Henry's reign, who made the translation at the request of his wife, Prudentia.

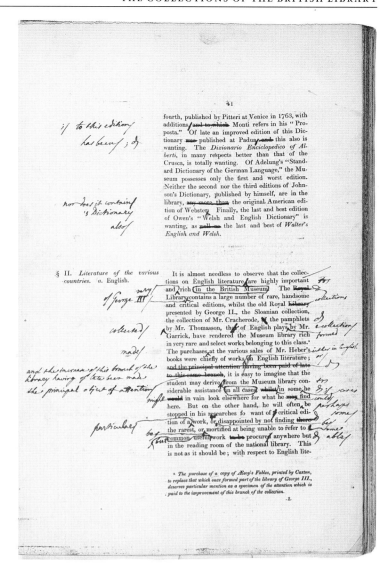

Above: The archives of the British Library contain a wealth of material for its history from the early 19th century – acquisitions, cataloguing systems, public services and administration. For the 18th century the necessary documents have to be sought in the archives of the British Museum. The illustration (far right) shows some of the amendments which Antonio Panizzi (Keeper of Printed Books, 1837–56) made to the proofs of his report of 1845 which argued for more funds to purchase books. It led to the Government increasing the grant for the purchase of books to £10,000, and the quadrupling of the size of the library in twenty years.

Left: This Manual of Prayers is thought to be the one carried by Lady Jane Grey to the scaffold on 12 February 1554. It contains in the lower margins her message of farewell to her father, the Duke of Suffolk, who was himself beheaded a few days later.

MAPS

The British Library's unrivalled holdings of maps, charts and topographical prints and drawings are found in four principal collections: the Map Library, Manuscripts, the Oriental Collections, and the India Office Records. Maps formed an important element in the foundation collections: the Cotton library held four thirteenth-century maps of Britain by Matthew Paris, as well as the Anglo-Saxon map of the British Isles (ca. 1000) and, in the Augustus maps and charts, a large proportion of the Tudor cartographic manuscripts that survive; the Harleian library had three fifteenth-century versions of Ptolemy's Geographia, and the Royal library had the Boke of Idrographie drawn for Henry VIII by Jean Rotz in 1542, and Lord Burghley's copy of Saxton's county atlas, the annotations in which show the value of maps in statecraft. Sloane's library contained many atlases, maps and charts dating from the sixteenth and seventeenth centuries, including works by seventeenth century chartmakers, and, in the Livro do Estado da India Oriental a magnificent visual and written record of Portugal's African and Asian empire in 1640. Manuscript and printed maps continued to be added to the collections, but the most important additions to the Library's map and chart collections came with the bequest in 1828 of George III's library (containing over 50,000 maps, plans and charts), and the libraries of Sir Joseph Banks and Thomas Grenville. The Beudeker collection of maps, views and prints of the Netherlands (1600–1750) was purchased in 1861 and is a unique source for the topographical history of that country. In 1880 the Frederick Crace collection of London plans and views was acquired. The collections of the British Library now contain over 3,000,000 maps, plans, charts, globes, prints, coasting pilots, atlases and aerial photographs, making it one of the largest in the world.

George III's cartographic and topographical collection brought with it manuscript drawings by Ordnance engineers – the precursors of the Survey proper – complementing the Library's virtually complete collection of all editions of the Ordnance Survey maps and plans, and the large collection of cartographic materials for eighteenth-century North America.

The most important collection acquired in this century was that of the Royal United Services Institution which included valuable maps relating to the Seven Years' War, North America, and theatres of war on the continent during the eighteenth century, the latter mostly Prussian in origin.

Thomas Boutflower's 'A Representation of the Mullet & Trout Fishery at the E. End of Byron's Sound in Falklands Islands' (West Falkland), [1768]. Maps do not have to be solemn, topographically accurate, or even skillfully drawn to be fascinating,

and the Library has hundreds of maps by 'amateurs' such as Lord Nelson, Lord Burghley – and Thomas Boutflower of Newcastle (1732–75). Boutflower, apparently a carpenter by training, served as a purser on board the sloop *Carcass* during its tour of duty with the

first British settlement on the Falklands between 1765 and 1768. He made his maps as souvenirs shortly before his return to England. This one shows the settlers hunting, shooting and fishing as they had to in order to survive in the swampy terrain of West Falkland.

Right: Depiction of Constantinople from Cristoforo Buondelmonte's 'Liber insularum Archipelago' (1420) as copied in Ghent or Bruges in 1482 for Raphael de Mercatellis, Abbot of St. Bavon, Ghent. The Library has many thousands of manuscript maps, charts, plans and atlases dating from Saxon times to the twentieth century. They cover all corners of the globe and an enormously wide variety of purposes. This map-view, from an early form of atlas of the Aegean and Ionian coasts and islands, was once owned by the famous connoisseur-collector, Thomas Howard, 2nd Earl of Arundel (1586–1646), and came to the British Museum, with others of his manuscripts, in 1830. Buondelmonte (c.1385–c.1430), was a Florentine humanist who spent much of his life in the Aegean. His 'Liber insularum Archipelago' was the precursor of a *genre*, the 'Books of Islands' or *Isolarii*, combining island maps, views and text and intended for travellers, seamen and geographers, that was to enjoy enormous popularity in the fifteenth and sixteenth centuries. This is widely recognised as being the most splendid surviving example.

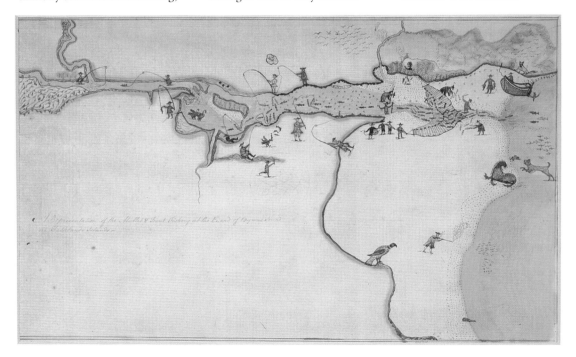

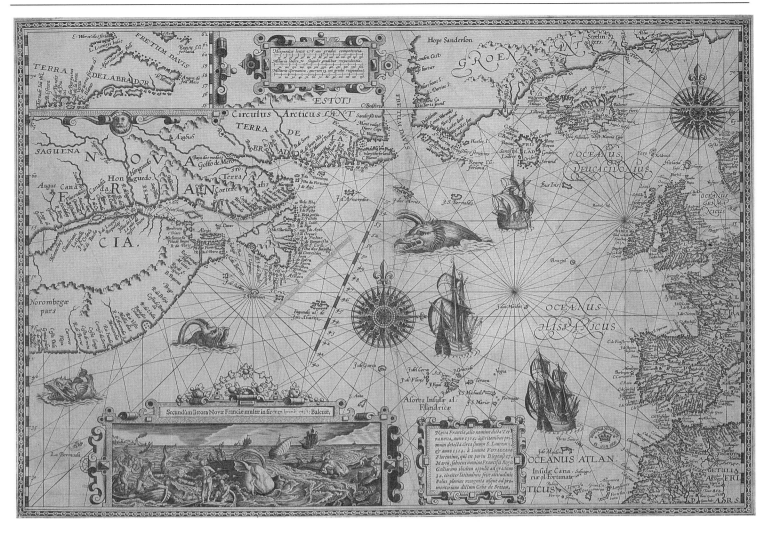

Above: Jan van Deutecum, 'Nova Francia', printed at Amsterdam about 1594. Among them is this map of the North Atlantic: one of the earliest masterpieces of the golden age of Dutch cartography. It includes up-to-date geographical information from Portuguese and English sources, a relatively factual depiction of whaling off Newfoundland, and it was probably used for navigation by the sea captains who laid the foundations for the Dutch sea-borne empire of the next century. At the same time the sea monsters, fantasy Atlantic islands, the ships and ornate compass roses convey the wonder of the age.

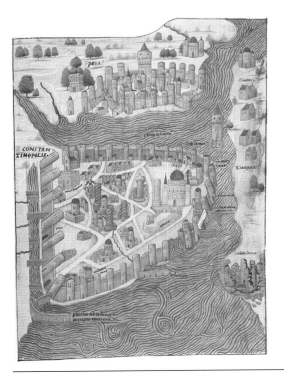

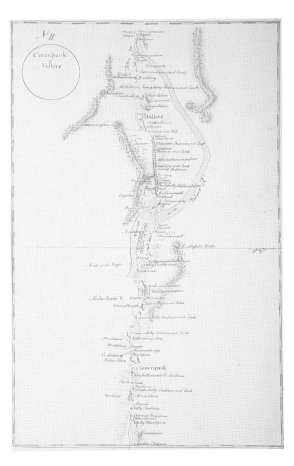

Right: 'Road from Avellore Chatrum by Cauveripauk and Vellore to Verringeveram', map 2 in 'The Roads from Madras (by the Pedanaig-droog Pass) to Bangalore; and thence by Sera and Chittle-droog, to the Toombudra River, on a scale of two British Miles to an Inch', by Captain Colin Mackenzie, Superintendent, Mysore Survey [1800]. Mackenzie's maps were the forerunners of the regular topographical surveys with which the survey of India filled the large-scale maps of the sub-continent in the nineteenth century. The India Office Records, with its manuscript and printed map collection, provides the official archive in London of this survey operation and the maps which derived from it.

Philip II of Spain (d.1598) was probably the original owner of the lavishly illustrated manuscript extolling the achievements of the reign of his father, Emperor Charles V, from which this gruesome picture is taken. It represents the involvement of Spain in the discovery of the New World. The miniatures in the book are based on a set of engravings published in Antwerp in 1556 by Hieronymus Cock. Although printing was already more than a century old when they were painted, there was still a substantial market for illuminated manuscripts among wealthy connoisseurs. More than two hundred years later the volume became the proudest possession of an English connoisseur, Thomas Grenville (d. 1846), whose incomparable collection was ultimately bequeathed by him to the British Museum Library.

ART

The Library's collections for the history of art from the eighth century to the fifteenth in Europe and the Orient are comprehensive, and representative examples can be seen in the exhibition galleries at Bloomsbury. Paintings, drawings and prints are to be found in every department. The chief strength of the collections is in the work of the French and Italian illuminators of the twelfth and thirteenth centuries, and the paintings from India which are to be found in the Oriental Collections and the India Office Library. To these pre-eminent collections can be added significant examples of religious and secular art from every known civilisation. Judaic, Islamic and Buddhist art are dominant, but there are impressive examples of art from the numerous cultures of North Africa, Asia and the Pacific.

For the period up to 1860, when the camera began to replace the artist, the Library's collections of topographical prints and drawings is the largest in Britain, and one of the largest in the world. For the history of British topographical drawing there are the remarkable collections of Samuel Grimm [3,000 drawings of English social life in the eighteenth century] and John Carter [45 volumes of architectural drawings].

An illustration for Book Eight of Homer's *Iliad* by the celebrated Italian artist Giorgio De Chirico for a lavish contemporary Italian edition of the Greek classic, printed in 1976. The work, translated into Italian by the Nobel prize winner Salvatore Quasimodo, was printed in a limited edition of which only 350 were intended for export. This edition was printed on hand-made paper, specially produced by the Miliani paperworks of Fabriano, and is bound in a contemporary Italian binding of black goatskin, decorated on the front cover with a specially commissioned gilt medallion by the sculptor Guido Veroi. De Chirico illustrated this work with a total of 26 separate plates. Since printing was introduced in 1465, Italy has excelled in the production of finely printed and exquisitely illustrated books. The British Library's collections of Italian fine printing are exceptional.

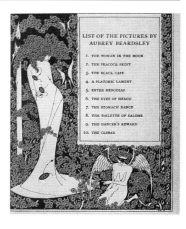

Oscar Wilde's *Salome* illustrated by Aubrey Beardsley is just one of the many notable items received by the Library under the provisions of the Copyright Act. The British Library inherits its position as a library of legal deposit from the Press Licensing Act of 1662, but it was not until a new Copyright Act of 1842, and its enforcement by Antonio Panizzi in the middle of the nineteenth century, that books began to arrive in significant numbers. By 1859 the number of items received by legal deposit exceeded 28,000. Today, the British Library's right to receive one copy of every publication distributed in the United Kingdom is based upon section 15 of the Copyright Act 1911. In recent years this has meant the deposit annually of approximately 350,000 separate items, including newspapers, magazines, maps and music, ranging from football programmes to limited private press editions, from children's books to complex scientific reports.

A lady visiting a shrine: a Mughal miniature, *c.*1740, by Muhammad Faquirallah Khan. Shortly after its founding, the East India Company's Library acquired in 1807 its most important collection of Indian miniatures and illuminated manuscripts from Richard Johnson, one of the Company's Civil Servants, who during his Indian career from 1770-90 had acquired over 1000 paintings mostly of the later Mughal and Provincial Mughal schools. Paintings in these styles form the main strengths of the India Office Library's collections of traditional Indian miniatures, of which the above is a fine example of the poetic and introspective styles current in the 18th century. Other miniatures have since been added, including the famous album compiled by Dara Shikoh, son of Shah Jahan, and given to his wife in 1642. These collections of 17th and 18th century miniatures, when added to the illuminated Indian manuscripts in the Oriental Collections, make what is probably the finest collection of such material in the world. Equally famous and important is the India Office Library's collection of Company paintings, paintings commissioned by British patrons from Indian artists, who modified their styles to accord with their patrons' general preference for watercolours and the use of European perspective and modelling.

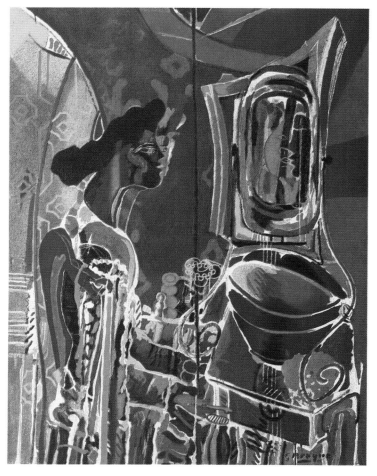

Ambroise Vollard's *Réincarnations du Père Ubu* with etchings and wood-engravings by Georges Rouault, Paris, 1932. This is one of the many French *livres d'artiste* in the Library's collections by artists as diverse as Braque, Derain, Dufy, Maillol, Matisse and Picasso. Ambroise Vollard (1865-1939) was a Paris dealer who published many *livres d'artiste* and who invented these satirical adventures of the grotesque and ugly Père Ubu in the colonies, at war and in the land of the Soviets, based on the original figure of Ubu in the play *Ubu Roi* (1896) by Alfred Jarry. Vollard commissioned the artist Georges Rouault (1871-1958) to carry out these etchings and wood-engravings which took Rouault sixteen years to complete. As in his paintings, the black contours of the figures here give an intensity and expressiveness to the illustrations, making this one of the artist's best works and a striking example of the *livre d'artiste*.

MUSIC

Although printed and manuscript music came to the Museum from the beginning, with notable examples from the Harleian and Royal libraries, no serious attempt to collect, organise, bind, and catalogue printed sheet music was made until the 1840s. Since then, however, the collection has been developed to a point where, with over 2,000,000 items, it may be regarded in its coverage as being the most comprehensive library of printed music in the world. It was especially fortunate that its expansion started at a time when important sixteenth-, and seventeenth-, century editions were still available for purchase. A particularly valuable part of the collection is the Hirsch library purchased in 1946 which, at a stroke, provided a collection of early editions of the Viennese classical composers that equals any other apart from Vienna itself. The reference collections in London are complemented by a substantial number of scores and collected editions of composers of many nationalities available on loan from the Document Supply Centre at Boston Spa.

The general collection of manuscript music is particularly strong in sixteenth- and seventeenth- century English sources and in the autograph manuscripts of modern British composers from Elgar and Vaughan Williams to the present day. While British music is naturally

The autograph of one of the best known of Schubert's songs, '*An die Musik*' written about 1817, forms part of the Library's Stefan Zweig Collection. Zweig Collection manuscripts range from a Bach cantata to Ravel's *Bolero*, and include works by Schoenberg, Berg, Webern, Bartok and Stravinsky. These scores supply a context to the great collection of twentieth century British music which in recent years has been the most important addition to the Library's general music manuscript holdings. The British Library now has extensive collections of autograph manuscripts of the leading figures in the regeneration of British music, such as Elgar, Vaughan Williams, Holst, Britten and Tippett, as the result of generous gifts. Other aspects of note in the general collections are the rich array of sources for English music of the sixteenth and seventeenth centuries, an important collection of manuscript copies of full scores of eighteenth century Italian operas, many of them unpublished, and one of the world's major accumulations of

late eighteenth and nineteenth century European musical autographs. Mozart's six 'Haydn' string quartets, Beethoven's sketch-book for the 'Pastoral' symphony, Rossini's 'Stabat Mater', Verdi's opera *Attila*, and

the late E flat *Rhapsody* for piano by Brahms are some of the better-known works in the last category. Collections like the Zweig, with its rich assembly of Mozart manuscripts, do more than add lustre to the music on display to

the public in the Library's galleries; they add to the strengths of the nation's scholarly resources built up patiently since the founding of the British Museum in 1753.

Folio 91 verso of the autograph manuscript of Handel's last oratorio *Jephtha*, composed in 1751. Handel was forced to break off composing, ironically in the middle of the chorus 'How dark, O Lord, are thy decrees', as his note records: 'bis hierher komen den 13 Febr. 1751 verhindert worden wegen relaxation des gesichts meines linken auges' [Reached this point 13 Feb. 1751. Prevented from continuing on account of the relaxation of the sight of my left eye]. He resumed 10 days later, but by 1753 he was completely blind. Almost all Handel's surviving autograph manuscripts are in the Royal Music Library. They were bequeathed by Handel to his friend and helper John Christopher Smith, who in turn presented them to George III in return for a pension of £200.

Bach's Cantata 71, 'Gott ist mein König'. The soprano part from a set of 19 printed parts of Bach's *Glückwünschende Kirchen Motetto* published in 1708. During his lifetime Bach's works circulated mainly in manuscript copies, and relatively few were actually published. As a result, the 220 or so surviving cantatas probably represent only about three-fifths of the total number composed, the other two-fifths being lost. Cantata 71 was the first work of Bach's ever to be printed, and the only cantata published during his lifetime. Only three copies are known to survive.

A page from the copy of the first edition of Debussy's *La Mer*, (1905) with his manuscript corrections and emendations. Most, but not all, of these were subsequently incorporated into the second edition of 1909. In bars 41-43 of the first movement, *De l'aube à midi sur la mer*, shown here, Debussy has strengthened the woodwind by indicating that the clarinets (third stave) should play an octave higher, in unison with the oboes, and has changed the bassoon part (fourth stave): instead of a single low held note on the second bassoon, both bassoons double the oboes and clarinets an octave lower. Debussy apparently omitted to alter the dynamic marking for the bassoons from *pp* (very soft, appropriate to the low held note) to *p* (corresponding to the oboes and clarinets). In the second edition this alteration has nevertheless been made, indicating that there must at some time have been a further stage of emendation.

a major emphasis, there are a significant number of autographs of the major European composers, among them J.S. Bach, Haydn, Mozart, Beethoven, Schubert, Schumann, Rossini, Verdi, Liszt and Brahms. There are also two outstanding special collections: the Royal Music Library, and the Stefan Zweig Collection. The former was deposited on loan by George V in 1911 and donated to the British Museum by Elizabeth II in 1957, commemorating the gift two hundred years earlier of the Old Royal Library by George II. It contains, in addition to autograph scores of Purcell, Alessandro Scarlatti and J.C. Bach, and the printed music collections of the Royal Family (especially of Queen Victoria and Prince Albert), an unrivalled collection of nearly one hundred volumes of autograph scores of Handel's works, presented to the Crown by the composer's heirs. The gift of the Stefan Zweig collection of musical and literary manuscripts in 1986 enhanced the holdings of composers' autographs in many areas, especially the great Viennese composers and European composers of the early modern period: Wagner, Grieg, Mahler, Schoenberg, Webern, Richard Strauss, Stravinsky, Ravel and Bartok. In 1988 the Library acquired by purchase from the Royal Philharmonic Society the manuscripts of the twelve 'London' symphonies of Haydn, written between 1791 and 1795 when Haydn visited London.

The loan collections at the Document Supply Centre include performance scores, books and periodicals on music, with acquisition emphasis on new publications, collected editions, and facsimile reprints.

Until the mid-nineteenth century music was mainly published from hand-engraved metal plates – a slow and expensive process. The invention of lithography at the end of the 18th century provided a much cheaper and quicker alternative, one eventual consequence of which was an explosion in the publication of cheap popular songs, often with splendid pictorial covers as in this example printed in Glasgow in 1869. The Music Library possesses an exceptionally rich collection of such pictorial covers, wide-ranging in both style and subject-matter. Quite apart from any intrinsic artistic interest, this particular example, like many others is of great documentary interest, illustrating as it does both the publishers' two Glasgow premises at 195 Sauchiehall Street and 49 Buchanan Street and also the type of omnibuses prevalent in the Glasgow of the late 1860s and early 1870s. An added point of interest is that, while topical subjects are common in the much more numerous London publications, such Glasgow scenes are comparatively rare.

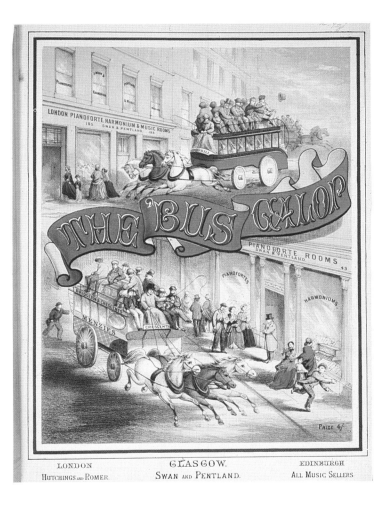

THE MAFEKING MAIL
SPECIAL SIEGE SLIP.

ISSUED DAILY, SHELLS PERMITTING.　　　TERMS : ONE SHILLING PER WEEK, PAYABLE IN ADVANCE.

No. 94　　　　Monday, March 19th, 1900.　　　　158th Day of Siege

The Mafeking Mail.

MONDAY, 19TH MARCH, 1900.

LATEST NEWS.

By the courtesy of the Colonel Commanding we are enabled to publish the following—

INFORMATION.

The party of cattle-looters who left here on Monday last, returned yesterday. They state that the Boers are very much vexed at the way that they have been treated by cattle-looters. They (the Natives) were unable to capture any cattle owing to the Boers making trenches round their cattle kraals. On their way back to Mafeking they were followed by a party of Boers, who overtook them near the Railway Siding near Madibi. The Baralongs made a stand and killed and wounded 10 of the Boers, and most of their horses. The Boers have now got the funks and are afraid to travel about the country in small numbers. They have informed the Natives that there is an army of about 1,000 Baralongs scattered about the country, and that there are hundreds of them near Madibi under British officers, with two Maxims ; also that they were going to move their Western laager to the Border. The Natives were also told, what we have already heard, about Plumer at Lobatsi, etc. The Boers would have taken all the Natives prisoners but for the protests of one Hartmann, a Zarp, who said that if they took away the Natives they would have to fight the Baralongs as well as the English, and that would mean "fighting an iron combined with a rock."

Four runners came in from Kimberley. They left Mafeking on divers dates and have been in Kimberley all the time waiting for the troops to arrive. They found the condition of the inhabitants of Kimberley much worse than ours, and they thought that the place was never going to hold out, as nearly everybody there was starving. It was very pitiful to see ladies and a lot of children running to the bottom of the diamond mines to take shelter against shell fire, and there were so many people that it made things worse.

Their relief came on February 14th, on which date the troops arrived. The Natives have no words to describe the number of the troops ; they think that the man who wrote the Bible referred to British troops when he said that there were many tribes among the Israelites and each numbered twelve thousand.

On the 15th the troops brought in thousands of Boers they had captured close to Macfarlanes, and later on they brought in Cronje and his army. On that day they ate ox meat for the first time.

They came back via Barkly West. The troops came via Fourteen Streams, and another lot went round via Barkly on the 18th February. They left this column at Pniel Mission Station. The Missionary there, together with four others, were taken prisoners and sent to Kimberley for stopping despatch runners. When the Boers heard that a column was advancing on Barkly, they waited three days, and then fled to Klipdam.

When they left Barkly they heard that troops were at Warrenton, and the Boers encamped at Fourteen Streams. The Natives say they cannot understand our troops ; when they find a number of wagons all they care about are rifles, forage, horses and cattle. They pour paraffin on everything else and burn it, including ammunition and foodstuffs. Before reaching Taungs they heard a heavy cannonade in they direction of Fourteen Streams, and they saw Boers who came from there hurrying back to their farms ; these Boers said they had given the fight to the English, but that they were still at the river.

At Maritzani they heard from one Dekooker, who went down last month to reinforce Jan Cronje, that Cronje himself was expected at his farm on Friday, and that the Boers were all crossing the Border.

A member of a cattle raiding party who left here last Saturday, also returned yesterday ; they were informed by Natives that the Boers had told them that Colonel Plumer had fought the Dutch, North of Pitsani, and defeated them with loss. The English had a fearful gun on the armoured train, which they used with great effect. Snyman's men left to reinforce the North on Tuesday, but the armoured train got to Lobatsi before them. The Boers informed the Native women that if they wanted to leave Mafeking they had better do so before Sunday as no people would be allowed to leave after that date. The Natives say they expect the Boers would be leaving before them, as Pitsani is not so far away from here.

The Native women (who told the Boers they were Gopani's people, stopped here by the war) have got messages from their Chief saying that the English had a laager near Gopani's, in the Transvaal, and they must be prepared to fly to the English with their arms as soon as there is an opportunity, for they had been armed against his wish.

Photographs for the Siege Exhibition.

We are glad to see that the Committee have eliminated all conditions in connection with Class 5, which were likely to prevent the holders of collections of photographs from exhibiting them. Now those terms at which so many objections were raised, have been withdrawn, we are sure none of those holders will be so selfish as to keep the garrison from viewing the most interesting record of events that modern science enables us to secure.

A SIEGE EXHIBITION

WILL BE HELD AT THE

MASONIC HALL,

ON

SUNDAY, MARCH 25th, 1900.

COMMITTEE :

Col. Baden-Powell ; Major H. J. Goold-Adams, C.B., C.M.G. ; C. G. H. Bell, Esq., C.C. & R.M. ; Capt. J. R. More ; F. Whiteley, Esq. (Mayor).

MANAGING DIRECTOR : J.W. De Kock, Esq.

HON. SECRETARY : J. R. Algie, Esq.

CLASS.

1. Prize, £5, presented by Col. Baden-Powell, for the Best Model of any locally manufactured Siege Weapon or Armament, or of any Fort or Redan.

2. Prize, £5, presented by Messrs. Wirsing Bros., for the Quaintest or Most Original Curio, ornamental or useful, constructed of any shells or bullets which have been fired into the town by the enemy during the Siege.

3. Prize, £5, for the best piece of Fancy Work made during the Siege.

4. Prize, £5, for the best piece of Lace worked during the Siege.

5. Prize, £5, presented by G. Riesle, Esq., for the best collection of not less than Forty Siege Photos.

And a Second Prize of £2 10s.

6. Prize, £5, presented by the Mafeking Mail, for the best Musical Composition, either Waltz or March. To be written for Piano only, or for Orchestra. The successful composition to be known as the "Mafeking Siege Waltz, or March."

7. Prize, £2 2s., presented by Major H. J. Goold-Adams, for the best Essay on Siege Life. Open to girls under the age of 15.

8. Prize, £2 2s., presented by Major H. J. Goold-Adams, for the best Essay on Siege Life. Open to boys under the age of 15.

NEWSPAPERS

The Newspaper Library's collections consist mainly of daily and weekly newspapers, including London newspapers from 1801 onward, English provincial, Welsh, Scottish and Irish newspapers from about 1700 onward, and large collections of Commonwealth and foreign newspapers. The Newspaper Library also houses one of the finest collections of popular periodical literature in the British Isles, including every type of magazine. Among the many unusual items held at the Newspaper Library are siege newspapers such as *The Mafeking Mail Special Siege Slip*. The siege of Mafeking during the second Boer War (1899-1900) is chronicled in this newspaper. It was published under the most hostile conditions and printed on any materials to hand, including wrapping paper and pages from account books.

The collections of newspapers, British and foreign, are contained in four locations: the Newspaper Library at Colindale, the main building in Bloomsbury, the Oriental Collections in Store Street, and the India Office Library. The total number of volumes exceeds 500,000, representing over 50,000,000 individual issues.

Until 1905 all the Museum's collections of newspapers were housed in Bloomsbury. Their origin in the collections can be traced to the Sloane library, but it is the collection of pamphlets, newsletters, and miscellaneous ephemera amassed by the London bookseller George Thomason which George III bought in 1762 and presented to the British Museum to which historians turn for the early history of the newspaper. Thomason's collection included over 7,000 individual issues of newspapers published in the period of turmoil between 1640 and the Restoration. In 1818 the Museum purchased the collections of the classical scholar Charles Burney, which included a unique collection of eighteenth- century newspapers, many from America, and also some of the earliest known examples dating from 1620. The early newsbooks and the Burney newspapers are kept at Bloomsbury.

Prior to 1869, when the deposit of newspapers under copyright began, the Museum acquired its newspapers through the Stamp Office. The regular deposit of London newspapers from the Stamp Office started in 1823, with provincial newspapers following in 1832, Scottish and Irish newspapers in 1848.

In 1905 the Museum decided, because of lack of space, to remove the English provincial, Welsh, Scottish and Irish newspapers to a new repository at Colindale. In 1932 new stacks and a reading room were erected at Colindale, and post-1800 London newspapers were sent there from Bloomsbury. The Colindale library has extensive facilities for the storage and preservation of newspapers, and a Reading Room which supports many ancillary services. The collections include over 250,000 reels of microfilm, of which a substantial proportion are of newspapers held in other libraries. A co-operative scheme (Newsplan) between the British Library and local county or regional library systems whereby all local newspapers held by both are microfilmed will add substantially to the collections, and contribute to the preservation of vulnerable materials. The Newspaper Library has, in recent years, added vast quantities of newspaper cutting files, including the biographical press clippings donated by the Daily Express – over 1,000,000 clippings referring to some 36,700 individuals.

The collections of foreign newspapers contain examples which do not survive elsewhere. Among the hundreds of curiosities are the single issue of Buffalo Bill's Wild West Courier (May 7, 1892) printed for the Earl's Court Exhibition, and the Daily Citizen of July 2, 1863, which was prepared by a Confederate printer but completed by Unionist soldiers after their capture of Vicksburg – printed on pages from a wallpaper sample book.

Newspapers from the countries of Asia in English and vernacular editions number over 1,500 titles. A comprehensive microfilming programme of oriental newspapers is in progress: filmed newspapers are held at Colindale, while a small number of outstandingly important issues is kept at Store Street. The India Office Library has an important collection of newspapers printed, for the most part, in Western languages in the Indian sub-continent.

Newspapers are increasingly being used by historians not only as evidence for the momentous events of history, but as a rich source of information for those forgotten events which represent the social history of the ordinary citizen. The Mafeking Mail Special Siege Slip – 'printed daily, shells permitting' – was printed on anything which came to hand, including pages from an account book, wrapping paper and note-paper.

MICROFORMS

The British Library's collection in microform (both fiche and film) of books, periodicals, overseas government publications, newspapers, scientific and technical reports, manuscripts and archives includes the full text of over 10,000,000 items. Microform texts are found in all departments of the Library, the largest collection being at the Document Supply Centre, which in addition to dissertations, doctoral theses, and translations, has 7,000,000 microfiches of technical reports issued by government agencies such as the National Aeronautics and Space Administration and the National Technical Information Service in the United States. Over 130,000 reports are added to the collection each year – the demand for microforms at Boston Spa exceeds 4,000 requests per week. The Newspaper Library holds microfilms of many hundreds of British and foreign newspapers, and Bloomsbury has over 2,000,000 titles in microform, a total which is growing rapidly as a result of agreements reached with the major microform publishers to deposit archival films of all material reproduced in the collections. On-going projects include the filming of all eighteenth-century items recorded in the Eighteenth-Century Short Title Catalogue, and the Nineteenth Century project. The entire output of the U.S. Government Printing Office since 1984 is available on microfiche. The British Library Information Sciences Service (Ridgmount Street) collection of microforms includes over 6,000 research reports, mainly from U.S. Government projects. The shelving required to accommodate the Library's microform collections exceeds forty kilometres.

PHILATELY

The origins of the British Library's philatelic collections go back to the bequest in 1891 of the collection formed by Thomas Keay Tapling, M.P. Consisting of over 50,000 postage stamps, together with a huge quantity of related philatelic items including postal stationery, postcards, lettercards, envelopes, etc. the Tapling collection is the foundation upon which has since been built one of the most important collections of stamps, fiscal and postal, in the world. The collection has been estimated now to contain over 8,000,000 'items', but since thousands of these 'items' are in fact sheets of stamps (varying from 4 to 240) it is more likely that the total is nearer to 40,000,000 individual stamps. Included in the collection, which is annually enriched by deposits from the Universal Postal Union in Berne, and the archives of the Crown Agents which contain unique collections of original artwork for the design of stamps.

The massive collection of revenue stamps, dating back to 1710, were deposited in the British Museum by the Board of Inland Revenue in 1966. The range of the Inland Revenue archive is wide, and covers stamps for taxes imposed as well as stamps for taxes which were never implemented (such as the match tax and the 'luxury' tax in World War I). The archive contains artist's drawings, trial proofs, die proofs and registration sheets and is the primary resource in the world for the history of British fiscal and postage stamps. There are several specialised collections donated in this century: the Row collection (1919) of Siam; the Fitzgerald collection (1947) of airmails; the Ewen collection (1949) of railway letter stamps; the Turner collections (1973) which includes duty dies from 1694 (supplementing the Inland Revenue collection which dates from 1710) and railway letter and parcel stamps; the Chinchen collection (1977) of Lundy Island material; the Scott collection (1977) of British airmail; the Murray collection (1980) for China.

An important collection of leaflets and advertising matter issued by postal authorities throughout the world provides a unique record of postal history.

The India Office Library has important material for the postal history of South Asia, and stamps which complement those associated in the Philatelic Collections.

Bhutan, a small kingdom in the Eastern Himalayas, has recently become known more for the stamps produced in its name than anything else. Unfortunately, a number of the issues produced in the past twenty years have been printed in quantities that have grossly exceeded the postal requirements, or have not been available to the public at face value in reasonable quantities. In spite of this, the Administration has been innovative in some of the material it has distributed, starting with an issue in 1967 for space achievements, which was printed and then the paper surface laminated with a clear prismatic-ribbed plastic coating, which gave the images a clear three-dimensional effect. In 1973, a set of miniature gramophone records were issued as stamps. The set consisted of five for ordinary postage and two for airmail use, and apparently are capable of being played on normal equipment. They have five items on different records, Bhutan History in both Bhutanese and English, two folksongs and the Royal Bhutan Anthem.

Right: Gilbert and Ellice Islands: 1969, 10 cents (Christmas); one of two pieces of 'rough' artwork produced by Jennifer Toombs in 1969, on the basis of a local design, and which shows a young Gilbertese woman and her child symbolising the Virgin and Child in a typical Pacific island scene. The strength of this design is emphasised by the clear Micronesian and Polynesian features of the young woman depicted. In this design the beach is shown as being sandy, but in the case of the 2 cents issue, the foreground is grass, the rest of the design being identical.

Centre panel left: Canada, 1927, 25 cents, London (semi-official); only seven examples remain of this reminder of a tragic attempted flight from London, Ontario to London, England. The flight, sponsored by the President of Carling Breweries Ltd, was undertaken by Captain Tulley, who left Harbour Grace, Newfoundland on 5th September 1927, and was never seen again. Captain Tulley was carrying 97 items of mail, each bearing one of the 100 special stamps which had been specially prepared for the flight.

Centre: India, 1854 4 annas (error 'inverted head'); errors arising from mistakes in the assembly of plates are not uncommon, but they have often given rise to the major rarities in philately. This is particularly so in this stamp. It was printed in two colours, the red frame being printed first. The error occurred when a few sheets were put through the printing press the wrong way round, resulting in the blue heads being printed inverted. It was twenty years before the 'inverted head' error was discovered and very few examples now exist.

Right: Jamaica, 1954, £1 (definitive); following the death of King George VI, and the subsequent Coronation of Queen Elizabeth II in 1953, many British colonial countries arranged for their definitive issues of stamps to be changed to bear the portrait of the Queen. In October 1953, the Crown Agents announced that an order had been placed to change the portrait on the current Jamaica £1 definitive stamp to that of the Queen. In March 1954, 2143 sheets, each of 30 of the new stamps, were despatched to the colony for use when the existing stocks had been sold. However, in February 1956, the Crown Agents announced that new definitive stamps had been ordered for Jamaica and these were released later that year. When

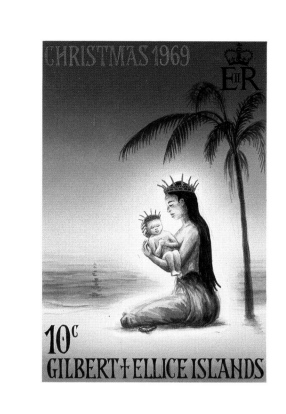

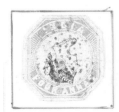

this new set was ordered, it was decided not to release the 1954 revised £1 stamps and to destroy them. But, in error, one sheet was sold and later recovered intact from the buyer. A block of four stamps, together with black proofs and a colour proof, exist today in the Royal Philatelic Collection at Buckingham Palace. A further set of black proofs and a colour proof are in the Crown Agents archives at the British Library.

Gilbert and Ellice Islands: 1971, 3 cents (New Constitution); although inscribed 2 cents, this piece of 'rough' artwork designed by Victor Whiteley was used for the 3 cents denomination, being one of two stamps issued to commemorate the New Constitution for the Islands. The design carries the inscription 'House of Representatives 1967 Legislative Council 1971' and shows the building in which the old House of Representatives convened. In 1976 the Ellice Islands separated from the Gilbert Islands, becoming independent, and changing their name to Tuvalu in 1978. In 1977 the Gilbert Islands became self-governing and, in 1979, achieved independence and changed their name to Kiribati.

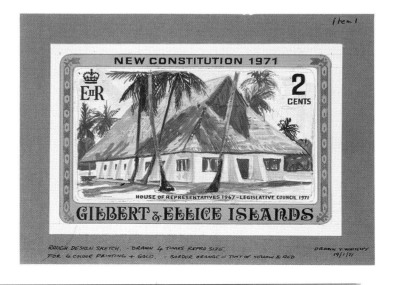

PHOTOGRAPHS

While it is clear that the British Museum Library did not collect photographs systematically, most of the departments do have substantial and important collections. They are found principally in the India Office Library (which has over 250,000), Manuscripts, the Map Library, and the Oriental Collections, though there are albums of photographs in the general collections of printed books. Canadian photographs for the period 1895-1924, received under Colonial Copyright, are unique, and there are significant photographs for the history of Malta. The Library's collections include a wide variety of books in which photographs were used as illustrations (before the invention of mechanical methods of reproduction) and these are being systematically identified and given preservation treatment.

Above: Landing goods near the Custom House, Calcutta *c.*1860, photographed by Samuel Bourne.

Below: Snub nose crocodiles at Magar Pir Talao, near Karachi, photographed about 1870 by Ritter Molkenteller and Co. Photographs held in the Prints and Drawings section number at present 819 collections, ranging from a single item to over 70 albums and comprising some 200,000 images. They date from the mid 1850s to the 1940s and include work by photographers such as Bourne, Beato, Tripe, Murray and the Tytlers. Early Indian photographers are also represented, amongst them Din Dayall, A. A. Khan and B. G. Bromochary. In all, over 400 photographers and photographic companies have been identified. The subjects cover every aspect of life in India, from historic events such as royal visits, viceregal tours and the work of border commissions, to picnics, parties and amateur dramatics, reflected in family albums. Views, studies of architecture, engineering projects, the military and portraits are also included. Several viceregal collections are held, the largest being that of Lord Curzon, mostly made up of formal presentation albums but often including personal photographs. The early photographs include some fine examples covering the immediate post-Mutiny period (*c.*1858), and an important part of the collection is formed by the original photographs made for the Archaeological Survey of India. These record sites and restoration work between the 1870s and 1922. To avoid unnecessary handling of the more fragile items a systematic programme of copy prints is being undertaken, and work on the photographs of the 1850s is almost complete.

THE COFFERED VAULT ABOVE THE DAIS IN THE T'AI-HÊ HALL.

Early photography captures the past in a way no other medium can do. Oriental Collections possesses several rare, early examples of the work of pioneering photographers. The image here of the Hall of Supreme Harmony in the Forbidden City, Peking, dates from the first decade of the twentieth century, and was taken by Japanese photographers. At the time, Puyi, the last Chinese emperor, was living in the Forbidden City, although he had been deposed in the Revolution of 1911. Other notable photographic collections include Sultan Abdulhamid's albums – 51 volumes of scenes of the late 19th century Ottoman empire, selected from the Sultan's voluminous collection of prints.

SOUND RECORDINGS

The National Sound Archive is one of the world's leading sound archives. It is a unique centre for the study of all kinds of music, literature, and the sciences, and a primary source for broadcasters, film-makers, theatre companies, advertising agencies, the record industry and the general public. Its collections include more than a million items on every format from wax cylinders and shellac discs to videos, DAT tapes and compact discs.

Copies of most current British commercial releases are deposited by the record industry. In addition to the large holdings of older records, there are also thousands of hours of unique unpublished recordings and a wide range of broadcast materials, many from the BBC Sound Archives.

The earliest recordings in the collections date from the 1890s, and include the voices of Florence Nightingale, Gladstone, Tennyson and Browning. There are recordings of Brahms and Joyce, and aboriginal chants from the Torres Straits collected by Sir James Frazer while writing The Golden Bough.

The recordings of music include classical, popular, jazz and traditional from every country. For the spoken word there is a wide range of recordings by twentieth century writers, especially those writing in English in Africa, the Caribbean and North America. The collections include live theatrical performances, interviews with actors, directors and playwrights, and other recordings associated with drama which are unavailable elsewhere.

The collection of recordings of wildlife sounds is the largest in the world covering over 5,000 species, and range from the earliest known (Ludwig Koch in the 1890s) to contemporary amateurs.

The reference library functions as an important source of information about all aspects of recorded sound, and provides a wide range of catalogues, discographies and other finding-aids, including catalogues of the sound archives of the BBC and the BBC indexes to song titles.

Above left: Columbia Graphophone, Type AZ, 1905, playing 2-minute wax cylinders. The National Sound Archive collections are principally of recordings, on original carriers and often also on tape copies. There is, in addition, a considerable amount of associated material; information on disc and cassette labels, sleeves and inlays is an important primary source for researchers, and the library has an extensive collection of record company catalogues, periodicals and publications relating to recorded sound. Artefacts are also an integral part of appreciating the ways in which recordings have been heard and understood. The National Sound Archive is therefore in the process of acquiring a major collection of phonographs, gramophones and other reproducing equipment from a life-long collector, Mr George Frow. Most are still in working order, and they will be both a valuable new facet of the Archive's research resources, and a focus for exhibitions.

Above right: Most listening at the NSA is through headphones, to which the recording is relayed from the playback room. The listener is able to talk to the playback staff by phone, and to consult documentation accompanying the recording. A cassette deck is available for anyone wishing to listen to a passage repeatedly – an actor working on a particular accent, for example. There are also facilities for listening over loudspeakers and for video viewing, as well as group listening and seminar rooms which can accommodate larger parties.

Below: Recordings are extremely vulnerable to interference and distortion, through flaws in either the recording process or else the carrier. The longevity even of Compact disks has been questioned, and certainly modern LPs can suffer from poor surface quality and are susceptible to damage. Fungal infestation, surface wear-and-tear, and breakages put

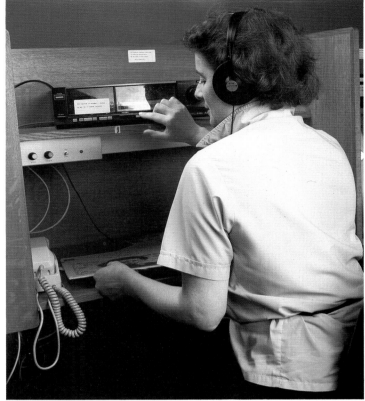

at risk a substantial inheritance of recordings on wax cylinders and acetate and shellac discs, and audio magnetic tape is similarly subject to deterioration from age and use. It is the responsibility of the Conservation Section to deal with such problems in the NSA collections. The desk pictured was designed to the NSA's requirements for a self-contained fully digital audio restoration unit. The capabilities of this Neve desk include low pass or high pass filtering to attenuate the extremes of the frequency spectrum; equalisation, allowing precise selection of the parameters for adjustment of the frequency response; notch filtering removing unwanted sounds; and limiting, compression and expansion where manipulation of a signal's dynamic range is required. New research sponsored by the NSA includes the development of CEDAR, a Computer Enhanced Digital Audio Restoration system running on a standard desk-top computer, and able to achieve remarkable improvements in sound quality.

The Library and its Users

The activities associated with collecting, preserving, and making available the wide range of materials necessary for research are complemented by a number of public activities which are intended to bring the Library and its users closer together. In addition to the specific services noted below, the British Library encourages active participation of its users in its affairs by an Advisory Council and a number of Advisory Committees for all the major departments of the Library.

ENQUIRY SERVICES

The most important of these are the fifteen public enquiry points in all of the Library's principal departments which deal with over 2,000 enquiries on an average day – by personal visit, by post, and by telephone. The enquiry desks are staffed by both curators with a wide knowledge of the collections and staff with specialist skills, who are there to assist all users in search of information, whether that information can be best satisfied from the resources available in the British Library or from other institutions. Enquiry points direct users to the best sources of information in the country, and taken as a whole, represent an important national information centre. In addition to the general enquiry points at Southampton Buildings and Kean Street SRIS has special services for business information and foreign patents, both with their own enquiry points, as well as Japanese information and biotechnology.

Right: To the North Library, built in 1934 to accommodate over 140 readers, authors, scholars and researchers come from all over the world to read rare printed books, sometimes in the only known copy, and other special or restricted material. Rare books can be studied here in conjunction with an unrivalled collection of similar and ancillary works. Reference books on bibliography and early printing are on the open shelves. Readers now use their own microcomputers in the North Library, and equipment such as comparators, watermark readers and ultra-violet lamps are available on request.

Left: The Enquiry Desk in the main Reading Room. Bibliographic enquiries from all over the world are answered here both in person, by letter and telephone. The desk is manned by professionally-qualified curatorial staff who advise readers on the use of the catalogues and other reference tools, and who have considerable knowledge of the Library's collections. Specialist curatorial staff can be called upon for advice when required.

The Newspaper Library attracts approximately 26,000 readers each year. These come from all walks of life and represent both amateurs pursuing personal interests as well as professionals who use the Library as part of their work. The collections are used to research a wide variety of subjects including family and local history, media studies, social and political history, and studies of particular events. There are 102 seats in the reading rooms, 32 of them for readers using microfilm. Facilities are also available for readers using typewriters, computers and tape recorders. The reference shelves contain the catalogues, a wide collection of newspaper indexes, press directories and a large number of books on journalism and the history of the press.

COMPUTER SERVICES

The British Library provides all users of the collections with access to the world's databases of information on the humanities, social sciences, science, technology and commerce. The three main service points for access to over 1,000 databases are at the Document Supply Centre, the Science Reference and Information Service and the Reading Room in Bloomsbury. Because of the overriding importance of having access to current information for those engaged in research in science, technology, medicine and business, the last few years have witnessed a remarkable shift from printed to electronic information sources. The Medical Information Service at the Document Supply Centre provides computer searching by expert staff of over 80 medical databases, as well as current awareness bibliographies distributed to subscribers worldwide. The number of databases currently available is being added to each year, and the British Library provides an essential service to its many users by means of its many computer search facilities, available in most of the reading rooms. The British Library also provides access to databases of information other than its own, including the University of London, the Library of Congress, and the National Library of Medicine. It has been estimated that computer databases provide cataloguing and indexing access to the equivalent of 1,000 kilometres of printed sources.

Scholars come from all over the world to work in the Manuscripts Students' Room, where original materials in western languages are available for study. On a typical day readers may be using Greek papyri, modern literary papers, mediaeval Latin charters, political records, and autograph music scores alongside some of the world's outstanding illuminated manuscripts such as the Luttrell Psalter.

PHOTOGRAPHIC SERVICES

Remote users requiring photographic copies of printed books and manuscripts account for the largest number of enquiries received by the departments of the Library. The demand for photographic and rapid-copy reproductions of materials in the collections is such that there are separate departments responsible for dealing with requests in the London buildings for copies of every type of document, manuscript and printed. Since the Photographic Service is also responsible for preservation filming in all the collections the number of images processed in a year exceeds 25,000,000. If to this total is added the photocopy requests received at the Document Supply Centre and the Science Reference and Information Service then the British Library's contribution to the information needs of the world exceeds 50,000,000 pages of text in any one year.

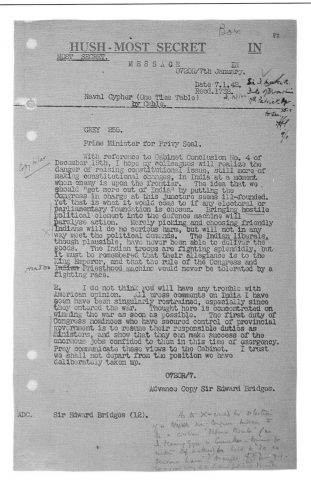

Left: 'Hush – Most Secret' telegram, 7 January 1942, from Winston Churchill to the Lord Privy Seal, Clement Attlee, deprecating any political concession to India: from the India Office Records, a vast archive occupying some nine miles of shelving and dating from the foundation of the East India Company in 1600 to the transfer of power to India and Pakistan in 1947 and to Burma in 1948. The Records include those of the Company, the Board of Control set up in 1784 by William Pitt to supervise the Company, and the India Office which took over from both Company and Board when the Crown assumed the Government of India in 1858. Focussed on the Indian sub-continent, but ranging also from the Middle East to the Far East, these archives provide an immensely rich source of original documentary material for the study of the political, economic and social history of the countries of South Asia, and the interactions of the British and South Asian peoples.

Right: The end of the Raj. Lord Mountbatten's final letter as Viceroy of India, 16 August 1947: from the IOLR's European Manuscripts comprising some 15,000 volumes or boxes of private papers illustrating the British connection with India. This growing collection dates from 1600 to the present day, and the persons represented range from Viceroys and Secretaries of State, through Governors of Indian Provinces, to members of the Indian Civil Service and their families, from Commanders-in-Chief to officers and privates of the Indian and British Armies, and from individual Indians and British scholars, missionaries, businessmen or travellers. Many of these private papers provide political insights into the official record, or depict the careers and social life of the British in India; some illustrate the varied commercial or cultural relations between the British and the lands and peoples of South Asia; while others reflect the viewpoints and reactions of the people themselves.

BIBLIOGRAPHIC SERVICES

From its inception in 1973 the British Library has recognised the need to provide services to one of its most important community of users – other libraries. In addition to the provision of information vital to the successful functioning of the nation's public and research libraries, the British Library serves as the collective national library resource for bibliographic information, and plays a leading role in enabling research into all aspects of the management of libraries and archives and the preservation of their collections.

The part of the Library concerned with Bibliographic Services is the national centre for bibliographic information in electronic form, maintaining a national database recording the output of British publishing, and providing the most important central resource of bibliographic records and services for the library community as a whole. Records created for the National Bibliographic Service are widely distributed and support key activities in libraries such as book selection, information retrieval, cataloguing and other technical processes. In addition to publishing the British National Bibliography (supplied to over 4,000 libraries worldwide), the British Catalogue of Music, Books in English, and Serials in the British Library, all of which form the national record of the printed word, this Department, situated in Novello House, is responsible for the Library's on-line bibliographic information service (BLAISE-LINE) used by over 950 libraries worldwide. The Library also supplies bibliographic records in electronic form for libraries to incorporate in their own computer systems. In 1988 over 20,000,000 records (from a variety of sources) were available to libraries in Britain, offering significant cost benefits over local record creation. By 1993, when the new building is opened, it is estimated that there will be on-line access to over 10,000,000 bibliographic records for the collections in all departments of the Library in addition to those from other sources. In 1987 the British Library became a participant in the Joint Academic Network (JANET) which links all university, polytechnic and research sites, thereby providing the Library with access to the on-line catalogues maintained by those institutions, and the research communities of Britain with simplified access to the electronic catalogues maintained by the Library.

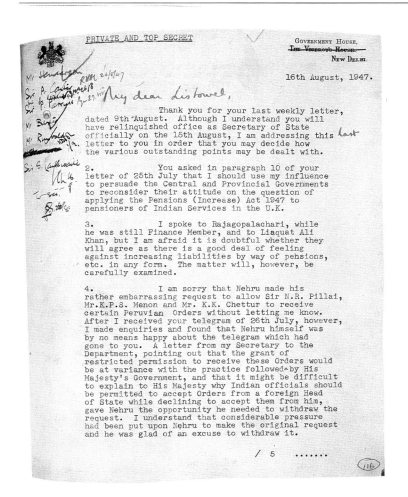

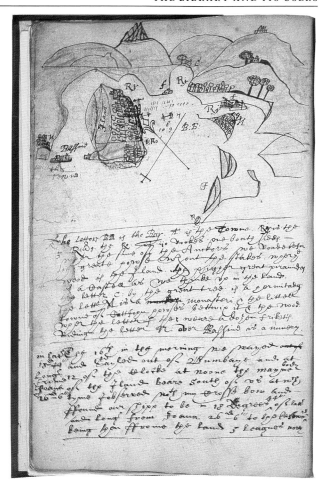

Above right: Sketch map of Bombay Harbour, by David Davis, in his journal of the voyage of the East India Company ship *Discovery* to India and the Persian Gulf, 1626-1629. The captain of each East India Company ship was required, on his return, to deposit at East India House the journal of his voyage. The resulting collection of over 9,600 volumes is an invaluable source for East India Company trading activity, navigation and shipboard practice in the seventeenth and eighteenth centuries.

Right: An illustration of electrical experiments from a copy of Luigi Galvani and Giovanni Aldini's dissertations on electricity and muscular movement (1792) presented by the authors to Sir Joseph Banks while he was President of the Royal Society. The Library's collections of Italian books form one of the richest and most extensive in any single Library – more than 1,000,000 individual items. Of these, the collection of books printed before 1501 is one of the largest anywhere, amounting to over 4,400 separate editions, of which some 100 editions are known to be unique.

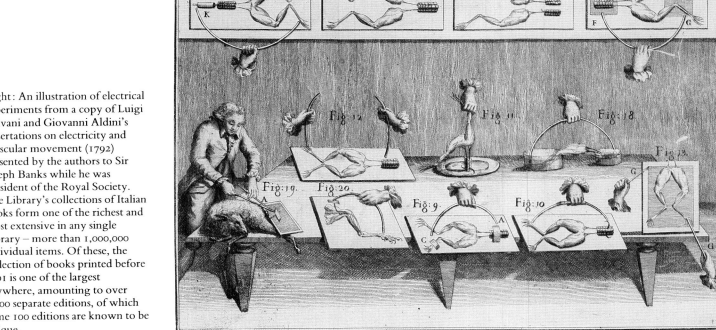

Research Services

The Research and Development Department funds and disseminates the results of a broad programme of research for the benefit of the nation's libraries, archives, and information systems, and their users. In recent years this has necessitated increasing involvement with the new micro-electronic technology, including the mass storage of information via electronic networks. The need for people to be adept at finding and using information for a wide variety of purposes led the Department some years ago to set up a research programme concerned with teaching information skills in schools. Specific activities being supported by the Department include the Library and Information Statistics Unit at Loughborough University, the Office for Humanities Communication at Leicester University, which has, for some years, been promoting the application of new technology to research in the humanities and social sciences through lectures, conferences, a widely-read Newsletter, and an online bulletin board available for users of the Joint Academic Network [JANET]; and the Centre for Bibliographic Management at Bath University, which has a broad concern with the generation, storage, retrieval and presentation of bibliographic records. Research and Development involvement at governmental level is crucial in determining policies which will affect the entire research community and the Department is closely involved with the Office of Arts and Libraries (the government department responsible for the British Library), as well as the Library and Information Services Council (LISC) and other national agencies. Liaison at the international level with appropriate agencies, for which the Department provides the Library's focus, is also of considerable and growing importance. The Department is a major source of the Library's annual output of publications, bringing to the national and international information community the fruits of research it has sponsored. The Research Reports, Research Papers, Research Reviews, Information Guides, British National Bibliography Research Fund Reports, and Annual Research Lectures are acquired as essential sources by libraries all over the world.

In addition to its support for research, the Library also, through the Research and Development Department, awards grants to other libraries and similar institutions for conservation, cataloguing and improving access to collections of national importance. At present awards for cataloguing are made from the Library's own funds, while awards for conservation and the purchase of significant items are made from the generous gift to the Library from the Wolfson Foundation and Family Trust.

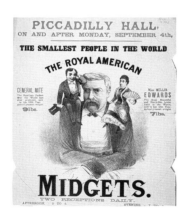

The Library has some notable collections of ephemera, which stand as testimony to the acquisitive spirit of private collectors. The Bagford collections of titlepages and fragments of printed books includes some 3,355 pre-1701 English titlepages, while the Ames collection numbers some 10,500 titlepages of printed books. The Library possesses a large number of playbills, of the eighteenth and nineteenth centuries, many of which originally were collected privately. The Evanion collection of pamphlets, handbills, posters, and trade cards forms a fascinating encapsulation of late nineteenth century English social life, and a rich resource for the history of popular entertainment.

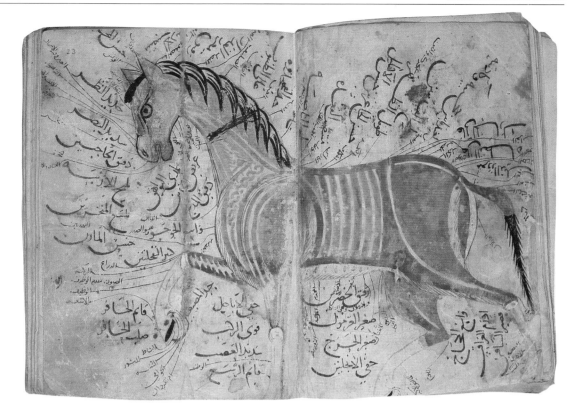

A double page illuminated illustration of a horse from an Arabic manuscript entitled *Kitāb al-Baiṭarah* by al-Azdī, copied in 620 AH/1223 AD, with annotations giving a full description of the perfect horse. Oriental Collections possess vast resources for the history of Eastern and Middle-Eastern science and technology.

A plate from Evelyn's copy of Andrew Snape's *The anatomy of an horse*, London, 1683. John Evelyn (1620-1706) like his fellow diarist Pepys, was one of the great English book collectors. His library survived, virtually intact, until 1977 when its dispersal at auction began. Thanks to the generosity of a number of benefactors the British Library was able to purchase 262 important items, most of those with Evelyn's highly individual annotations. A representative Evelyn collection thus joined some of the great collections of printed books which form the basis of the Library's claim to be the National Printed Archive. The Old Royal Library, built up by English monarchs from Edward IV onwards and greatly augmented after the Union of the Crowns, important in its own right, also brought with it the privilege of copyright deposit. The Thomason Tracts, the exhaustive collection of printed material issuing from the London and provincial press between 1640 and 1660, acquired on publication by a London bookseller, George Thomason (d. 1666) and described by Carlyle as 'the most valuable set of documents connected with English history ... for informing the English what the English were in former times:' were bought by George III who presented them to the British Museum in 1762. Three notable bequests were David Garrick's collection of plays in 1779, the fine books of C.M. Cracherode in 1799 and the natural history library of Sir Joseph Banks in 1820. Surpassing these, both in quantity and quality, were the books of Sir Thomas Grenville (1755-1846) described as 'the noblest bequest to the nation (not excepting Sir Hans Sloane's) ever made by a private person in this country'. Most magnificent of all, the King's Library, assembled by George III during his long reign, was presented, after some persuasion, by George IV in 1823, and is still housed in the noble room built for that purpose in 1828. Of these collections only Thomason and Garrick are exclusively 'English', but such is their combined strength in holdings of material printed in these islands from Caxton to the end of the eighteenth century that by the mid nineteenth century, the British Museum Library had become the world's principal repository for such material – a position consolidated by constant and judicious acquisition and inherited by the British Library with all its concomitant responsibilities to the world of scholarship.

Exhibitions and Educational Services

Exhibitions are an important element in demonstrating to the general public the breadth and importance of the Library's collections, and the first permanent exhibition of printed books dates from 1851, the year of the Great Exhibition. The main exhibition galleries are in the Bloomsbury building, but exhibitions have always played a part at the India Office Library and Records and the Science Reference and Information Service. On view in the Bloomsbury galleries are manuscripts illustrating the history of Western handwriting and illumination, literary and historical autographs, music manuscripts, manuscript maps, oriental manuscripts, and a wide range of materials for the history of writing and the history of the book in all languages. Following the tradition of exhibitions devoted to events and writers established in the last century (Luther in 1885, Gibbon in 1894, the Nelson centenary in 1905, the tercentenary of the King James Bible in 1911, Shakespeare in 1923), there have been since 1973 a number of major exhibitions which have drawn on the resources of many of the Library's departments: The American War of Independence (1977); The Christian Orient (1978); Russian Futurist Books (1978-79); Wonders of the Age [Persian miniature painting] (1979); The Benedictines in Britain (1980); Famous Books in the History of Science (1982); Japanese Popular Literature of the Edo Period (1981-82); The Art of the Book in India (1982); Virgil (1982-83); Renaissance Painting in Manuscripts (1984); St. Augustine (1986); Wonders of Creation [natural history drawings] (1987); All the King's Men [the Revolution of 1688] (1988). The major exhibitions are complemented by a regularly changing series of smaller displays commemorating the work of writers, artists, musicians and book designers. The publications (leaflets and catalogues) of these exhibitions are written by experts in their field and represent a considerable corpus of scholarly and readable information for the public about the Library's collections. The permanent exhibition cases in the Grenville Library the Manuscripts Saloon and the King's Library are intended to give the visitor an instructive sample of the whole range of the collections.

The Document Supply Centre offers extensive services to its visitors. Some 2,000 people a year are shown round the Centre. The tour shows how the DSC works and handles requests. A discussion with a senior member of staff can usually be arranged for parties with particular interests. Over 3,000 people a year use the Reading Room, which holds a representative collection of reference books, bibliographies and the more important abstracting and indexing publications on open access. Advice and assistance is available from professionally qualified staff.

Left: A conservator adjusts the position of a 16th century Nepalese manuscript of the great Hindu epic, the *Mahābhārata*. Amongst the Oriental material on permanent display in the King's Library are the world's earliest printed book, the *Diamond Sutra* (dated AD 868) and manuscripts written on vellum, paper, tree bark, palm leaf, bone, bamboo, and even silver and gold.

Below: A curator putting the final touches to the graphic centre piece of the special exhibition, 'All the King's Men', commemorating the tercentenary of the Glorious Revolution of 1688. The first temporary exbitition was mounted in 1851 to coincide with the Great Exhibition, and the galleries have housed a permanent display of the Library's treasures since the late 1850s. The Library currently mounts five to six temporary exhibitions each year and plans a major exhibition each year in the much increased gallery space which will be provided in the new building at St Pancras.

Complementing the exhibitions in the Bloomsbury galleries. which attract millions of the public (British and visitors from overseas) every year, is the Education Service which organises lectures, seminars, tape-slide presentations and videos for audiences of all ages. These initiatives demonstrate the Library's determination to acquaint visitors with the richness of its resources for the public good, and consider their various needs, interests and tastes. The several departments of the Library actively seek to promote their collections in a variety of ways: international colloquia to explore means by which the Library can contribute to research in American, Canadian, Australasian, Indian and Asian studies; seminars for users of the specialist collections; training courses in the retrieval of electronically stored information for scientific, humanistic and commercial data; active participation in national and international bodies concerned with information on every subject; introducing the next generation of the Library's users to its fundamental importance as a cultural asset. The Centre for the Book, begun in 1988, plans to bring to a wide spectrum of the general public, as well as specialists, the extraordinary resources which the British Library possesses through lectures and seminars. The new building will make many of these activities easier to organise as it will provide facilities, supported by advanced audiovisual technology, unavailable in a building constructed in the last century.

A Philatelic Society seminar. As an extension of the daily departmental work, the Philatelic Collections, on application, arrange special evening meetings for societies. Societies can arrange for the attendance of up to twenty of their members for a one and a half hour meeting, during which they are given a talk about the Library's philatelic collections and a commentary on the material which is displayed for their interest. The material displayed is carefully selected to cater for the particular interests of the visiting society, from collections which are not normally on public display, and those attending are given the opportunity to examine the material closely and to ask questions about it and the service which the Philatelic Collections provide to students for personal access for research. Lectures and seminars are an important part of the Library's educational function.

Library Services

Above: The Library provides users with a comprehensive photographic service, ranging from colour transparencies to xerographic copies. In an average year the library supplies users with over 3,000,000 images in addition to over forty cameras dedicated exclusively to preservation filming of books, periodicals and newspapers in a fragile condition.

As a national library the British Library works in close association with the Library Association of the United Kingdom (founded in 1877), and provides indispensable services to libraries of every type and size – there are few libraries which do not benefit in some way from its activities – and to individual librarians as members of the Association. From its inception there have been important links with the Library of the British Museum, and these have been maintained and strengthened in recent years. Internationally, the Library plays a leading role in the International Federation of Library Associations, and its responsibility for the reference and loan collections of the Library Association – the British Library Information Sciences Service – freely available to all members, illustrates one of the many ways in which it serves the information needs of the nation. The library has a comprehensive collection of books, serials and leaflets on libraries and their management from many countries, and publishes a newsletter (Current Awareness Bulletin for Librarians and Information Scientists) providing librarians everywhere with readable (and frequently entertaining) digests of what has been recently published on all aspects of librarianship. In addition to a wide variety of publications associated with librarianship (in all languages), the library contains over 1,000 periodicals, report literature in microform, theses and dissertations, audio-visual materials, and trade literature. The reference collection is available to any member of the public, though only members of the Library Association and staff of the British Library are entitled to the full range of services provided.

Events at the National Sound Archive have embraced subjects ranging from wildlife recording techniques to radio soaps, classical composers to pop videos, Black British jazz to literary recordings. Speakers include academics, broadcasters, critics and performers – Laurie Taylor, Victoria Glendinning, Juliet Stevenson and Courtney Pine are among the better known names on some very august panels. Events provide a unique opportunity to explore different aspects of the collections, and to instigate serious discussion of major issues such as the future of broadcasting. The Spring of 1988 saw a visit by eight Bulgarian musicians including the Trio Bulgarka, a remarkable female vocal ensemble. Following the great success of their first two albums, they came to bring their music to a wider audience in Britain, and at the NSA discussed and demonstrated their stunning vocal polyphony and instrumental techniques to a full house.

The British Library Bookshop in the Grenville Library, British Museum Building was opened in December 1988 by the writer, broadcaster and former British Library Board member Magnus Magnusson. It stocks a wide range of titles on subjects related to the Library's collections – book arts, cartography, history, literature, music, religion – as well as cards, gifts and children's books. Many of the books on sale are the Library's own publications, which include bibliographies, reference works and an increasing number of colour-illustrated introductions to the collections on display in the exhibition galleries. The shop was designed by Insight Design Services of Welwyn Garden City and has over 100 metres of shelving, eight racking panels and eight triangular showcases for special promotions. On average more than 200 customers are served from its single counter each day, a very high number for a bookshop of this size.

Publishing Services

The British Library is an important publisher of scholarly books, with a range of bibliographical publications which only a handful of publishing companies can rival. The publications of the British Museum Library, which began with the printing of the Statutes and Rules in 1757, are to be found on the shelves of every research library in the world, but the Library is now as concerned to publish books of interest to the general reader as to researchers in the many disciplines for which the collections are a primary source. Many of these books have won awards for their high standards pf design and production. The Library's publications, most of them compiled by scholars who are experts in their field, now constitute a library of information for whole communities of users, from the researcher who needs to know what his colleagues are investigating (Current Research in Britain, covering all disciplines, compiled at the Document Supply Centre) to the librarian who needs to know the latest discoveries in information technology (the Research Papers published by the Research and Development Department), just as users depend on electronic publishing to enable them to find references to the most recent article on AIDS or the latest book on the economy of Malaysia.

The range of the Library's publications is as wide as its collections. In addition to specialist guides the Library publishes numerous catalogues in printed and microfiche form. For the sciences and technology the catalogues of the Science Reference and Information Service and the Document Supply Centre have a world readership: Books at Boston Spa (all monographs published since 1980), British Reports, Translations and Theses, Index of Conference Proceedings, Scicat (books and serials held by SRIS), &c. Bibliographic Services publishes many aids to cataloguing (name authority and subject lists) which are indispensable to other libraries, as well as the definitive listing of British books (the British National Bibliography) and the British Catalogue of Music.

In 1959 the National Lending Library for Science and Technology, the precursor of the Document Supply Centre, undertook to sponsor translations of selected Russian journals. This series is still in progress with translations of journals dealing with chemistry, mathematics, steel, thermal engineering and welding.

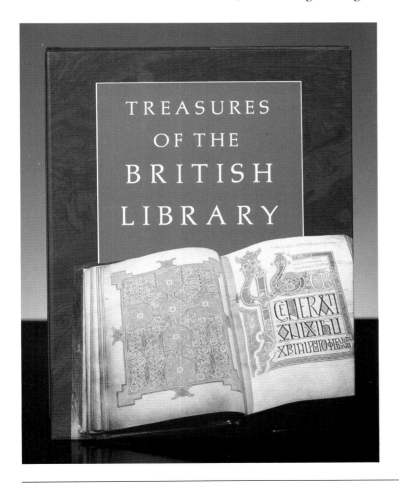

Treasures of the British Library, the latest and largest volume in a growing list of colour-illustrated books based on the Library's collections. The Humanities and Social Sciences publishing office also produces regular 'tie-ins' with special exhibitions in the Great Russell Street galleries. All general-interest titles are available through booksellers in the United Kingdom and many overseas countries, as well as in the Library's own shop in the Grenville Library. A full list of publications is updated annually and can be obtained free of charge.

Access to the Collections

The size and variety of the total collections of the British Library are such that no single catalogue could satisfy the needs of its many communities of users. From the first attempt at a printed catalogue of the books in the British Museum Library in 1787 to the present day the Library has published both general and specialist catalogues covering all types of material in its collections – printed books and manuscripts of all periods in various languages, maps, prints and drawings, music, newspapers, patent and scientific literature and sound recordings. Over three hundred such catalogues have been published, and there are many in preparation. Since 1976 the Library has pioneered the creation of bibliographic access to its collections by undertaking primary responsibility for the creation of the largest historical union catalogue ever undertaken – the Eighteenth-Century Short Title Catalogue – which will, by the year 1994, record in electronic form over 300,000 eighteenth-century books, pamphlets and single sheet items based on the collections of over one thousand libraries throughout the world. For modern books the Library maintains numerous electronic catalogues covering the whole output of British publishing since 1950; scientific literature held in the Science Reference and Information Service; monographs, serials and conference proceedings published since 1980 at the Document Supply Centre; books acquired for the general collections in Bloomsbury from overseas in over four hundred languages; maps; music; and manuscripts. There are plans to convert many of the existing catalogues to electronic form, thereby providing access in ways which printed catalogues by their nature deny. By 1993, when the new British Library will be opened to the public, it is estimated that over 10,000,000 electronic records will be available for the various kinds of flexible access which computerised catalogues permit. The most important of these electronic catalogues will be the General Catalogue which, ever since its first appearance in print a century ago, has been an indispensable bibliographic tool for research libraries everywhere.

In addition to publishing catalogues in printed and electronic form the Library's specialist departments maintain hundreds of unpublished indexes and handlists, thereby facilitating access to the collections. To such catalogues and indexes as the Library has been responsible for publishing there are hundreds more published by individuals and institutions which record British Library holdings. The extent of these aids to research is such that it would require a substantial volume simply to list them.

The British Library's Copyright Receipt Office is responsible for acquiring copies of British publications for the National Printed Archive and receives over 300,000 titles each year. These include monographs and periodical parts, printed music, maps and atlases, government publications and newspapers. Machine-readable information is created for legally deposited material and is available to users around the world – in print and microform, directly downloadable or on magnetic tape for loading into local computer systems, and online through the BLAISE databases. Over the years a programme of national and international co-operation supported by the latest developments in telecommunication technology has made British Library catalogue records accessible through overseas networks, whilst information from other national libraries and commercial bibliographic utilities are available through the British Library's National Bibliographic Service.

Training is a key element of the support offered to subscribers of BLAISE online services. Over 200 people a year attend the regular courses held in Sheraton Street's fully-equipped Training suite. These cater for all levels of proficiency – from the complete beginner to the online expert. They attract attendees from all the groups represented in the user-base including academic, public and special librarians as well as a growing number of 'individual' subscribers. Courses are also run, upon request, at users' own sites. For those unable to attend a course, the *self-starter* training package, designed to be run on a user's own microcomputer. offers a local alternative. This is complemented by an online Training File, offered at a reduced-access cost, a full range of documentation and a Help Desk service.

Below: The ESTC Editorial Office. The Eighteenth Century Short Title Catalogue was begun in the British Library in 1976. The project is recording the output of British and British colonial presses in any language and English language printing wherever it was produced, 1701-1800. It is the largest retrospective cataloguing project in the world. In 1979 editorial centres were set up in America to process the holdings of North American libraries. The office in the Library handles the reports of libraries of the UK and the rest of the world. Altogether there are over one thousand institutions, which range from national and university libraries to record offices and regimental museums, contributing to the project. The methodology pioneered in the Library, which is an enhancement of internationally agreed systems of cataloguing modern books, has been accepted around the world. The terminals pictured here are linked to the Research Libraries Group's computer, based in California, on which the American team also works. The Research Libraries Information Network (RLIN) is an inter-active computer cataloguing facility and the ESTC team is the first in the Library to work directly online to the file it is creating. The experience gained in this initiative is assisting the development of the BL's own cataloguing system.

Above: A demonstration to scholars of the ESTC online file. From time to time the Eighteenth Century Short Title Catalogue runs demonstrations of the uses to which the online file can be put by scholars working in the period. The aim is to introduce researchers to the vastly enhanced access to data that the computer provides. Records can be retrieved by keywords in almost all areas of the description and by locations. Once the retrieval capabilities of BLAISE-LINE are understood it is possible for scholars to conduct searches locally or through the search service in the Reading Room. Libraries everywhere are recognising that the enhanced access offered by computerised catalogues will revolutionise the way in which research is conducted in the Humanities.

Preservation

The size of the British Library's collections and the diversity of the materials they contain present problems not only of scale but of complexity, and the Preservation Service, established as a separate department in 1983, is responsible for the largest library preservation initiative in the world. The librarian today must reconcile two conflicting responsibilities: providing access to collections indispensable for research, and ensuring their preservation for future generations. As the volume of material at risk inexorably increases, and the number of users requiring access similarly increases, the custodians of research collections face difficulties for which there are no historical precedents.

Preservation problems arise from both intrinsic and external factors. Excessive use, careless handling and poor storage conditions all play a part in hastening decay, but the most important and least visible enemy of a book or document lies within its covers. Paradoxically, older books and manuscripts on paper made from rags are in very good condition; more modern books, particularly from the period 1860-1900, are crumbling to dust because of the chemical instability of their wood-pulp paper. Of the millions of items in the British Library's collections twenty-five per cent of the pre-1850 books and sixteen per cent of the post-1850 books need conservation treatment, largely due to paper-embrittlement. Each year more books become endangered; inevitably some will not be rescued in time.

The Preservation Service is responsible for the overall direction of conservation and preservation services throughout the Library. Conservation and repair work is carried out by the Library's own specialised and highly-skilled staff, at the London-based conservation bindery (one of the largest in the world), conservation studios for Manuscripts, Oriental Collections and the India Office Library and Records, the National Sound Archive, and a repair unit at the Document Supply Centre at Boston Spa. Outside contractors are also used to deal with backlogs of books which require treatment.

A curator preparing Giovanni Simonetta's *Sforziada*, (1490) for loan to the exhibition 'The Sforza Court: Milan in the Renaissance' in three separate venues in the United States, in the Winter and Spring of 1988–9. Incunabula are books printed between the time of the invention of printing, *c.*1450, and the end of the fifteenth century. In the eighteenth century they were particularly favoured by the great collectors who were then active, and to whose encyclopaedic interest the British Museum owes its existence. Important collections were formed from books that had formerly belonged to monastic houses or noble and royal courts, whose fortunes had changed in the immense turbulence of European history during the eighteenth and early nineteenth centuries. Many of these books found their way to great national collections, either by acquisition of such collections en-bloc, or after they had filtered through auctions, the book-trade and newly-formed private collections. The British Museum was richly endowed, both by its foundation collections and later, by the very choice collections brought together by King George III and Sir Thomas Grenville, which were offered to the nation in 1823 and 1847. With purchases added steadily and judiciously the British Library has a magnificent collection, representing more than a third of what survives of European printing in the fifteenth century, a proportion unsurpassed by any other collection. It is thus that the British Library could contribute significantly to the travelling exhibition which showed the riches of the Milanese court of the Sforza family. Shown here is the preparation for transatlantic transport of the book known as the *Sforziada*. Its text was commissioned by the Milanese dynasty for its glorification and confirmation of its power; it was translated from the original Latin of G. Simonetta into Italian and printed in Milan in 1490, at a time when the power of the dynasty was under threat. The book was acquired by the Library with the collection of Thomas Grenville. The richly illuminated opening page is reproduced on the back cover of this book.

Below: The familiar printed book is not the only material which requires conservation treatment. The library's manuscript conservation studio has responsibility for the repair and preservation of Oriental treasures in a wide variety of formats and materials, not usually encountered in Western libraries. The Burmese manuscript pictured here shows the royal procession of King Minden and his army and court officials to dedicate the kyauk-taw-gyi Buddha image at Mandalay, and was painted in the mid-nineteenth century. The joints in this folding panorama had weakened and split after repeated folding and the panels were in danger of becoming separated. Considerable skill was required to insert new paper joints to strengthen the manuscript, allowing it to fold without damage. Conservators can be called on to repair materials ranging from ancient Egyptian papyrii to medieval illuminated miniatures. The Library's conservation studios have an international reputation, and are committed to promoting excellence in the treatment of special materials.

With the enormous collections which the Library holds, significant backlogs of preservation work exist. In all areas, much more material requires repair than it is possible to treat. Choices and priorities are made on a planned basis. The aim is to achieve a balance between the needs of repair for the most important items which are in the poorest condition and the need to develop programmes of work to which the Library can commit resources over a considerable period of time. The Library estimates that its backlog for the treatment of printed books is in the region of two million volumes.

The Library meets its conservation needs in a variety of ways. It possesses its own in-house bindery and conservation workshops. These undertake the most demanding repair work, requiring high levels of craft skills and experience which can take many years to develop. Each year the Library fully repairs the paper and bindings of some 30,000 printed books, and dozens of thousands of Western and Oriental Manuscripts. Boxing of valuable material is done to prevent damage, with some 6,000 volumes being boxed each year. Some 75,000 volumes of the London collections are treated each year.

One very important initiative concerns detailed planning in the event of disaster from fire and/or flooding. Preparation and training are vital in ensuring a speedy response in the event of a disaster, so that staff can be deployed effectively and losses minimised. A near-disaster occurred at the Document Supply Centre in December 1987, when a burst pipe caused flooding which damaged over 10,000 Russian books. A salvage programme was quickly effected and various techniques (including blast-freezing and vacuum freeze-drying) succeeded in rescuing almost all the damaged books.

The Preservation Service supports research into technical conservation problems and treatments, and recent projects have studied the causes of foxing in paper; the use of aluminium salts on bookbinding leathers; the potential use of gamma irradiation to kill fungi; and the problems of removal and reversibility of adhesives. Investigations at the University of Surrey into paper strengthening and de-acidification by a graft co-polymerisation technique have proved successful, and the process is now being adapted for bulk processing of brittle books. Other research has taken the Library into the forefront of new technology, with the development of two new methods of conservation copying: the overhead photocopier, and the electroluminescent copier. With this equipment almost any book, however fragile, can be copied – without damage – for readers.

The dilemma created by the need to preserve original documents and books while satisfying the needs of users is most easily resolved by the provision of substitute copies. Preservation microfilming in the Library has been undertaken on an unprecedented scale, and many collections now must be consulted only on this medium, though access to originals can sometimes be granted by special arrangement.

Digital storage of source material, both for documents and recordings, holds the promise of economy and rapid access, and the newly installed Neve Desk at the National Sound Archive is the world's first digital signal processing unit developed for archival purposes. Capable of handling both analogue and digital input, it enables the Archive to transfer recordings to a digital medium on which signal deterioration will not occur. The conversion of documents, printed and manuscript, to digital storage may replace microfilm as a medium for the preservation of materials which continued use will inevitably destroy.

The Preservation Service encompasses a wide range of activities united by a single aim: ensuring the survival of a documentary heritage which is the envy of the world. The issues are complex, and resources, financial and human, are inadequate. In addition to the primary responsibility for preserving the collections the Library established in 1985 the National Preservation Office, which plays an important role in assisting other libraries with their preservation problems as well as publishing information on new techniques to deal with the deterioration of paper and book materials.

Trusteeship of the past is an onerous responsibility, and meeting the challenge requires imaginative thinking, a sound understanding of the needs of those engaged upon research into the past, and not a little courage.

The British Library possesses outstanding collections of photographs. Those in the India Office Library and Records amount to some 200,000. There are many thousands of prints reflecting the work of the early pioneers incorporated in printed books alongside text. The Library possess a collection of some 3,000 early Canadian photographs, many of which are known to be unique. From the beginnings of photography, the striving for image permanence has been the quest of many distinguished photographers. However, the methods of making and developing negatives and positives were often experimental in the early years of the science and did not meet with uniform success. Fading of images has remained a constant problem resulting in very significant conservation problems today. Additionally, poor quality paper and backing materials have contributed to the deterioration of images. A start has been made on a photographic conservation programme in the India Office Library and Records, but it is not possible to conserve more than a few hundred images each year owing to the pressure of other priorities for conservation staff. The greatest possible care is taken to preserve the integrity of the original image, and to retain the sequence in which photographs are grouped together, often in photograph albums.

Hand repair of leaves, deacidification of leaves, sewing of leaves and the Surrey Process. The durability of paper is often taken for granted. However, it ages like all other objects. The fibres of paper contain a certain proportion of water, and this reacts over time adversely with atmospheric pollutants such as sulphur and nitrogen to break

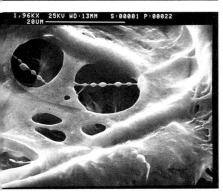

down the fibres. The problem of aging has been added to on a world wide scale with the production of poor quality papers, often derived from wood. Current conservation techniques can greatly extend the life of certain papers with the use of deacidification. To accomplish this is a time consuming process. Books have to be taken apart and each leaf placed in a specially prepared solution. The paper receives additional protection against further ageing by acids. Each leaf of the book is dried and the leaves are placed back together again in their original sequence. Many thousands of leaves printed and manuscript, are further supported by the attachment of very thin transparent tissue to hold tears in the paper together. Where leaves have had paper torn away replacement paper is attached to

the torn leaf. This calls for skill in the matching and attachment of the torn edge with the new portion of paper, with the aim of making the attachment as unobtrusive as possible. For many thousands of leaves more, it is necessary after deacidification to support the whole leaf to permit future use. This is done by placing thin sheets of transparent tissue, coated on one side with adhesive, onto the original sheet and then fixing the tissue to the sheet with dry heat. Printed books and manuscripts have to be resewn and

a new binding made to protect the repaired text. Older printed books and manuscripts have their section sewn back together again with the sewing being woven around cords. The cords then are attached to boards which protect the text. The Library is developing a large scale programme of deacidification and paper strengthening. Whole books will be treated simultaneously without taking the books to pieces. The paper fibres will be coated with polymer after treatment, allowing use for far longer than would otherwise be the case.

1899 Jubilee edition of Pushkin's *Lay of the Wise Oleg*. Watercolour illustrations by V.M. Vasnetsov and text handwritten by V.D. Zamirailo. Reproduced by lithography. The late 1890s heralded thirty years of extraordinary diversity and originality in Russian book design. The British Library has a supremely rich collection of illustrated books and journals from this period, ranging from elegant editions of symbolist poetry illustrated by artists from the World of Art grouping, savagely colourful satirical journals from the time of the 1905-07 revolution, Futurist books and pamphlets of the 1910s, to Constructivist books and architectural journals of the 1920s. Most of this material is both very rare and very fragile, and presents a variety of complex preservation problems. This work came to the Library loose: the paper was extremely brittle, and in danger of complete disintegration. The restoration of this item involved: testing the paper to determine how acidic it was; testing the inks to see how much they might run if aqueous deacidification were to be carried out; deacidification of each leaf; hand repair of each leaf, using materials of good quality sympathetic in colour and texture to the original paper; placing the leaves in their original order. Leaves have been put together to form a frieze, and the edges had to be strengthened with thin strips of tissue to effect this.

Support for the British Library

While its fundamental activities are supported by Government, the British Library recognises the importance of what Sir Thomas Bodley, founder of Oxford University's library, called the 'stirring up of men's generosity'. That is done not only by encouraging collectors to bequeath their treasures for the national good, but by direct initiatives.

The American Trust for the British Library was formed in 1979 with the aim of enhancing the Library's American collections, the largest outside the United States. The Trust's primary objective is to fill gaps in the Library's collections for the period between 1880 and 1950 in all subjects. In the period up to the end of 1987 the Trust succeeded in raising over $2,000,000. The origins of the remarkable collection that now inspires the efforts of the Trust can be traced to an earlier joint venture between Panizzi and the American bookseller Henry Stevens of Vermont. Between 1846 and 1866, the year in which Panizzi retired as Principal Librarian, Stevens had placed more than 100,000 American books in the Library, and was able to claim by the 1880s that the British Museum 'contains today probably the largest and best collections in existence of American history and literature.'

In 1987 the National Preservation Office launched the 'Adopt a Book' scheme, whereby companies and individuals can sponsor the preservation of particular books in urgent need of skilled treatment. Many hundreds of books have benefitted from the public response to this appeal. The enormous task which the preservation of our heritage presents is one in which all who share our belief in its permanent value must be given an opportunity to assist.

In 1988 the Library sponsored the launch of the Friends of the British Library. The purpose of the Friends organisation is to bring together those for whom the continued existence of a great national library is a matter of fundamental importance, and to enable them, as members, to get to know it better. They in turn are encouraged to help both to widen public understanding of the Library and its role as a cultural centre and guardian of the national heritage, and also to create greater awareness of its contribution to science, technology and industry. The Friends will provide a channel for seeking additional financial support to aid the Library's development at a time when its finances are severely over-stretched. The Friends arrange lectures, and discussions on the work of the work of the Library and other relevant topics; schedule social events, including special private views of exhibitions; and publish a regular newsletter.

The British Library's preservation problems are not unique. But they are serious. How can the cost of a necessarily wide range of preservation and substitution options be met from a budget which is declining year by year? The Library is committed to and expert in preservation but its resources are inadequate. At least 2 million items in the national collections are in need of repair, and the number grows daily as some 8 miles of new material is added to the collections each year. The Adopt a Book appeal asks the nation to help save its literary heritage by paying for the restoration of an item which is in a serious state of decay and, often, can no longer be issued to readers. A donation of £200 pays for full treatment; the donor receives an illuminated scroll and a bookplate in the restored volume notes the adopter's name. All contributions are welcomed and all donors are told of the title their money has helped to save. Hundreds of books have already been saved through the appeal. Their restoration has been undertaken by craftsmen using the traditional skills of conservation and binding. Materials used are carefully selected to ensure they are sympathetic to the style of the book and will not cause it further damage. Once work is completed on the volume it can again become part of the working collections of the British Library.

The Future

The British Library, given its resources for an understanding of the past, the present, and what we choose to make of the future, has no parallel in any country. It nourishes invention and curiosity; it provides for the needs of industry and commerce, without which national prosperity withers; it sustains research, without which there can be no progress; it possesses the documentary sources for the evolution of thought in all countries at all times, without which we would be deprived of history. Before the invention of writing when history was an oral record, handed down from generation to generation, its custodians were honoured above all. Millennia later, libraries preserve that tradition. Among the many thousands of libraries throughout the world, the British Library is pre-eminent in its determination to serve those institutions and individuals for whom information is an imperative, to preserve the heritage of knowledge, and to demonstrate its belief in the unity of knowledge and the benefits which flow from such a belief

Millions of people all over the world benefit from the British National Bibliographic Service. Students and researchers keeping up to date in their subject areas, MPs making decisions, schoolchildren carrying out project work, businessmen tracking down vital sources of information, pensioners choosing leisure reading. Helping them in their quest for information, education or entertainment are the countless libraries and research centres in this country and overseas – public libraries and academic libraries, libraries in schools and colleges of higher education, government libraries, commercial, industrial, professional and national libraries. Libraries using the information and services created and distributed by the British Library to help them locate the information their users need.

Chronology

1753   The founding of the British Museum.

1757   The first publication of the British Museum. The Old Royal Library given to the nation by George II.

1759   The British Museum opens in Montagu House.

1762   George III bought and presented to the nation the Thomason Tracts [1641-1661].

1787   The first printed catalogue of the British Museum Library.

1799   The collection of Clayton Cracherode given to the nation.

1801   The India Office Library founded [became part of the British Library in 1982].

1817   The Museum acquires the French Revolution tracts collected by Colin, Marat's publisher.

1818   The Museum acquires the collection of Charles Burney.

1820   The natural history and science library of Sir Joseph Banks is given to the British Museum.

1825   The gift of Sir Richard Colt Hoare's collection of Italian printed books. The Museum acquired the oriental manuscripts of Claudius Rich, and is bequeathed the Chinese and oriental books of John Hull.

1828   The Library of George III (given in 1823) is received at the British Museum.

1831   The Museum acquires the first part of the French Revolution tracts acquired by John Croker [the second part was acquired in 1856].

1837   Antonio Panizzi becomes Keeper of Printed Books [Principal Librarian from 1856 to 1866].

1842   The Copyright Act which ensured that all British publications were deposited in the Library.

1847   The bequest to the British Museum of the library of Thomas Grenville.

1855   The founding of the Patent Office.

1857   The present Round Reading Room opened to the public.

1867   The creation of the Map Library.

1885   The Patent Office Library founded [now part of the Science Reference and Information Service].

1891   The bequest to the Museum of the philatelic collections of Thomas Keay Tapling.

1892   The creation of the Department of Oriental Printed Books and Manuscripts [now the Oriental Collections].

1898   Francois Chevremont, Marat's biographer, presents to the Museum seventy volumes of works by, and about Marat.

1902   The Patent Office Library Reading Room opened.

1905   The newspaper collections moved to Colindale.

1910   The bequest to the Museum of fifty books acquired by the father of Alfred Huth chosen by the Trustees.

1911   The Copyright Act which ensured the deposit of maps, charts and atlases. The deposit of the Royal Music Library by George V.

1914   The North Library [the rare books reading room] opens.

1916   The Central Library for Students founded [later the National Central Library, now the Document Supply Centre].

1930   The Central Library for Students becomes the National Central Library.

1937   The British Museum acquires the library of Thomas James Wise [the Ashley Library].

1946   The Hirsch Music Library purchased.

1949   The British National Bibliography founded (first issue in January 1950).

1960   The British Museum given the responsibility for setting up the National Reference Library of Science and Invention.

1962   The founding of the National Lending Library for Science and Technology [now the Document Supply Centre].

1965   The Office of Scientific and Technical Information founded [now the Research and Development Department].

1966   The Patent Office Library incorporated in the National Library of Science and Invention.

1968   The gift to the Museum of the collection of bookbindings collected by Henry Davis.

1973   The creation of the British Library.

1977   BLAISE, the first U.K. online bibliographic service established.

1982   The India Office Library and Records becomes part of the British Library.

1983   The British Institute of Recorded Sound becomes part of the British Library [now the National Sound Archive].

1986   The Stefan Zweig bequest of musical and literary manuscripts.

1988   The Library Association Library becomes the British Library Information Science Service.